D0406128

EARTHQUAKE!

YOUR CHANCES • YOUR OPTIONS • YOUR FUTURE

IAN MACDONALD AND BETTY O'KEEFE

CAVENDISH BOOKS
VANCOUVER

First published in Canada in 1996 by

Cavendish Books Inc.,
Unit 5, 801 West 1st Street,
North Vancouver, B.C. V7P 1A4
Phone (604) 985-2969

Copyright Ian Macdonald and Betty O'Keefe 1996

Canadian Cataloguing in Publication Data

Macdonald, Ian, 1928-
  Earthquake!

  ISBN 0-929050-60-6

1. Earthquakes - British Columbia - Lower Mainland. 2.
Emergency management - British Columbia - Lower Mainland
3. Disaster relief - British Columbia - Lower Mainland. I.
O'Keefe, Betty, 1930 -   II. Title.
HV551.5C3M32 1996   363.3'495'0971133   C96-910519-3

Kobe earthquake photographs were taken by Dr. John Sherstobitoff.
Cover photograph by Tony O'Keefe.

Printed in Canada

CONTENTS

CONTENTS – CONTINUED

FOREWORD

This book was written to inform the residents of southwestern British Columbia what could happen when a strong earthquake strikes. The text is based on the opinions of experts in many fields who shared their concerns and explained what they are doing to prepare for what they consider to be the inevitable.

The information was obtained by reading and research as well as from interviews with geologists; engineers; representatives of phone, gas and electrical utilities; police and firefighters; hospital officials, volunteer organizations; transportation and transit staff; dam and water supply experts; port and airport officials; municipal, provincial and federal authorities; broadcasters and many others who responded generously as well as a few who didn't.

A recent upsurge in earthquake activity around the world — from Turkey and Greece to the Ring of Fire countries around the Pacific — leads some to believe that B.C.'s turn may be sooner rather than later.

ABOUT THE AUTHORS

Ian Macdonald has worked on the *Victoria Colonist*, the *Vancouver Province* and the *Vancouver Sun*. He was legislative reporter for the *Sun* in Victoria for five years and Bureau Chief in Ottawa from 1965 to 1970.
Later he became Director General of Information for Transport Canada. While in this position he developed and scripted a film which took a silver medal at the New York Film Festival.

Betty O'Keefe was a reporter on the *Province* for seven years and later supervised corporate communications for the Noranda group of companies in Western Canada and the Western U.S. During this 15 year period she wrote two short books, *Brenda — The Story of a Mine* and *The Mines of Babine Lake.*

In 1994, Macdonald and O'Keefe decided to combine their talents for writing books.

Their first joint venture was published in May, 1996, and is entitled, *The Klondike's 'Dear Little Nugget.'* A second, book, *An S.O.S. from Vanderbilt Reef* is expected shortly and *Earthquake!* is their third collaboration.

Damage to port facilities in Kobe

AN EARTHQUAKE ON THE MOVE

In a few million years, Planet Earth will be a chilly, lifeless dot, floating in the vastness of a cold, dead galaxy. It's a long time, however, before the lights go out and today Earth is a lively spot which generates a lot of heat and action. It's a sphere with a fiery, molten middle and a half-baked crust that expands, contracts, rises, falls and crumbles fairly frequently. Perched a-la-mode atop one of the crumbliest bits is the coast of British Columbia and particularly susceptible to the rumblings from inner earth are the Queen Charlotte Islands, the Lower Mainland area of Vancouver and Vancouver Island.

A real rattler of an earthquake is on the way. Geologists, seismologists and other scientists, engineers and geotechnicians agree that the B.C. coast is prime earthquake territory and there's a big one on the way although they don't know exactly when or where it will strike. The small Seattle shake on May 26, 1996, was classified as a lowly 5.4. on the Richter scale. The quake in Kobe, Japan in January, 1995, was a 6.8 and that was more than 10 times stronger because the Richter scale is logarithmic. It could be said — "You ain't felt nothing yet."

Making no bones about the future, Dr. Garry Rogers, Head of Earthquake Studies at the Geological Survey of Canada's Pacific Geoscience Centre in Sidney, B.C., suggested a large earthquake off the west coast of Vancouver Island, perhaps as high as nine on the Richter Scale, is not just possible, it's inevitable and it's not if, it's when. Rogers also said: "A Kobe, Japan sized earthquake under Vancouver would be much worse than a stronger earthquake off the coast. As in Kobe it could result in damage in the hundreds of billions of dollars. It would be the worst disaster in Canadian history." Rogers explained that the floor of the Pacific Ocean is on the move forcing its way under the North American continent. This results in a lot of seismic activity and one day will cause what is known as a subduction earthquake.

The "Big One," as scientists call it, would be larger and longer than the more frequent intra-plate quakes which continually send tremors along the

B.C. coast, largely unnoticed but with the potential to shake us up at any time. A big one has occured in the past every 300 to 800 years and could cause significant damage to some large structures even though it would be centred some 150 kilometres west of Vancouver, off the coast of Vancouver Island.

WEST COAST EARTHQUAKE HISTORY		
Year	Location	Magnitude
1872	Washington/B.C. border	7.4
1899	Yukon/Alaska border	8.0
1918	Vancouver Island	7.0
1929	Queen Charlotte Islands	7.0
1946	Vancouver Island	7.3
	Most damaging quake in Western Canada	
1949	Queen Charlotte Islands	8.1
	Largest quake ever recorded in Canada	
1949	Washington	7.0
1958	Alaska/B.C. border	7.9
1964	Alaska	9.2
	Tsunami damage on Vancouver Island	
1970	Queen Charlotte Islands	7.4

No matter if it's the big one or a direct hit from an intra-plate quake centred near Vancouver — years away or as you read this — in a matter of seconds the world as we know it will come tumbling down, buildings and bridges will collapse, tunnels cave in and dams burst. There'll be floods, landslides and tidal waves. Gas line breaks will trigger raging fires which cannot be controlled because water lines are broken and roads impassable. Broken electrical wiring will spew sparks in the air and transformers will explode. Thousands could be killed or injured, and as an aftermath survivors face public panic, a massive search for the wounded and the dead, outbreaks of disease, breakdowns in social behaviour, financial loss, public exodus, financial ruin and years of rebuilding.

Robin Gardner, until recently Vancouver's regional representative for the Provincial Emergency Program (PEP), was critical of the status of many earthquake preparedness and recovery plans in the Lower Mainland warning that without good plans and practice, "a 20-second shake can result in a 20-year recovery period." In today's world no one can wait 20 years, particularly when it has been demonstrated in some devastated areas that the recovery period can be shortened.

Bob Lee, Assistant City Engineer and Emergency Planning Coordinator for Coquitlam, stated succinctly: "Apathy only happens when people don't understand the problem. The biggest hazard any of us face is an earthquake. If we don't systematically upgrade buildings and facilities we will be bankrupt. We should also not forget that in the Lower Mainland we could have raging forest fires in the midst of everything else."

The duration of an earthquake will seem like the longest few seconds of your life. You could lose your equilibrium and have trouble standing.

Kobe: Port facilities suffered heavy damage

An Earthquake On the Move

Beliefs in "solid as a rock" are shattered and "terra firma" can even liquefy. In earlier times, people feared an earthquake was the end of the world. Today, survivors of any sizeable quake describe it as the most frightening experience of a lifetime. Often the noise is deafening. What once was safe and secure is no more and even when the earth is still again your body may be trembling in shock.

What do you do? Where do you turn? Phone lines will be down and 911 may not answer. Following the recent small tremor near Seattle, many Vancouver phones went dead because they were overused and emergency lines were jammed with needless calls. Following a bigger shake even cellular phones are not expected to function as everyone tries to dial out at once. If you don't have a battery radio you won't hear emergency measures broadcasts with information that could save your life or make it easier. It is difficult to imagine the cities of Vancouver or Victoria, modern metropolitan areas with sophisticated and fairly efficient infrastructures, suddenly without the services that are a part of everyday life.

If you're in a devastated area, family, co-workers or neighbours will be the only immediate help you have to aid in the recovery process. Experts say you're probably on your own for the first 72 hours and maybe longer depending on the amount of devastation.

How ready is southwestern B.C. for such a disaster? If fate is kind the big one won't strike for ten years when the Lower Mainland should be in better shape to handle such a disaster. To quote one of today's emergency preparedness experts, there are "little clusters of keenness" and great "black holes" where there is too little planning and coordination is next to nonexistent.

In 1995, a long overdue decision was made to bring order to the 20 municipalities that make up the sprawling Greater Vancouver Regional District (GVRD). Funds were found to support an earthquake preparedness coordinator for a two-year term. She is Ruth Harding of Vancouver who has her own emergency planning business. She began her two-year appointment in October, 1995, and is looking at the regional situation from the top down, to define exactly who is responsible for what and who has authority to act. Some of the areas being examined closely by Harding and others are communications, water supply, and the availability of structural engineers to examine buildings and large structures in the post quake period.

Preparedness has traditionally been affected by public apathy and a shortage of funds. There is always a more urgent civic need than preparation for disaster which might happen sometime in the future. Strapped for cash, local politicians have heard as clearly as their federal and provincial counterparts the public chant for "No more taxes." They also know that if

RECENT QUAKES IN THE RING OF FIRE

June, 1996	The Aleutians, Alaska	7.7
May, 1996	Munroe, Washington	5.5
March, 1996	Nootka Island, B. C.	4.9
October, 1995	West Coast, Mexico	7.6
September, 1995	Mojave Desert, California	5.5
August, 1995	Off Coast of Chile	7.8
March, 1995	Sakhalin Island, Russia	7.5
January, 1995	Kobe, Japan	6.8
March, 1994	Bogata, Columbia	5.7
January, 1994	Los Angeles, California	6.4

something goes wrong the chant will change to: "You should have known. Why didn't you prepare for this?" The experts know that fire is the greatest aftermath of an earthquake, yet in downtown Vancouver four firehalls are in the high-risk category, likely to collapse or be badly damaged and out of action. Lack of funds is holding up their replacement.

There has been a proliferation of quakes around the world recently and warnings from authorities have improved awareness of the impending danger in B.C.

One of the most noticeable effects is the millions of dollars spent recently upgrading bridges in Vancouver. Also, by the year 2,000 the National Building Code, which provides building standards for Canadians, will impose stricter regulations on construction of all kinds in the Lower Mainland.

The insurance industry, after a significant, in-depth study offered a gloomy forcast of death and destruction from a quake affecting B.C. Industry leaders admit that covering the repair costs would be impossible. A shingle shaker wouldn't be a problem, a major quake would. Insurers are making a concerted effort to cooperate with government, business and the public to probe the whole question of earthquake risk and insurance. The cost of recovery after a major earthquake is staggering. The study states that a tremor measuring 6.5 on the Richter scale in the Lower Mainland area of B.C. could run up a bill of more than $30 billion. Admittedly, that's only an educated guess and the actual figure would depend on how and where the quake struck. In the Los Angeles quake of 1994 a large slab 18 kilometres underground moved upwards creating a 6.7 earthquake. It killed 60 people, destroyed or made uninhabitable 3,000 homes, including apartments, townhomes and single family dwellings; buckled 10 highway bridges and knocked out three major freeways. The bill was more than $20 billion U.S. and the same thing could happen here.

The partial destruction of Vancouver and the surrounding area would have a devastating economic impact, not only on the province but on the whole country which relies on B.C. as a major contributor to the national economy, one of three provinces which make equilization payments to poorer regions. The province has 13-percent of Canada's population, contributes more than 13-percent of the gross domestic product and pays about 14-percent of the personal income taxes.

An Earthquake On the Move

After a large quake or even a smaller one centred on Vancouver, damage to the port, airport and other transportation links could effectively stop the flow of goods across Canada and to other North American destinations with crippling results. One preparedness official estimated an earthquake in the Lower Mainland could effect as much as 30-percent of the total economy of Canada.

The underlying problem in coming to grips with this potential disaster is a fatalistic, laid-back, lack of concern by most of the population. Many feel the chances of it happening are about the same as their chances of winning the 6/49 lottery. There is a feeling that it won't happen and if it does it's years away. This type of thinking influences about 70-percent of the population of the Lower Mainland who don't even carry mimimum earthquake insurance. They might be influenced by a shake that set highrises swaying, homes rattling and produced minor power failures, without death, injury or significant financial loss, say the experts who point out that we've had only the odd little shake in recent times. There are, however, hundreds of small earthquakes every year that go unnoticed. Emergency centres report they do get many calls from citizens whenever there is a large quake anywhere in the world, or a little rumble in the neighbourhood, often from newcomers to Canada, those who have experienced earthquakes elsewhere. Fortunately, some are concerned enough to take steps to help themselves.

Within the GVRD's 20 municipalities, five areas have created full-time emergency preparedness positions employing in total about 15 people. These areas are the City of Vancouver, the North Shore which includes North and West Vancouver, the Tri-Cities area encompassing Port Moody, Coquitlam and Port Coquitlam, Langley and Richmond. Among those assigned part-time duties are several fire chiefs and other municipal officials who have developed plans for survival and recovery, but the degree to which they have been tried and tested varies greatly.

The glaring inadequacy is the absence of a comprehensive area-wide, quake-resistant communications system. Many of the communities in the GVRD could not talk to each other because their systems are not compatible. Recent experience in California and Japan has demonstrated that this is an essential component for survival and recovery. Former Provincial Attorney General Allan Williams, who currently sits on West Vancouver Council, was quoted recently saying: "Somebody at the regional level, with the as-

Ham radio operators would play a big part in maintaining communications after a severe earthquake

sistance of the attorney general, should sit down and say, 'Look you guys, get your act together. Decide on the kind of radio communications system you want and set it up.'" And he was only talking about the lack of communication between police departments.

At the present time hundreds of ham radio operators with battery sets have offered their services and would play a big part in emergency communications following an earthquake. There are also encouraging signs that an overall plan for the area is moving forward.

Among the best organized to meet the threat of a major earthquake are the public utilities, for obvious reasons. They deal with breakdowns on a daily basis and are essentially always in an emergency mode. If they can't restore service, reactivate the phone system, supply gas and electricity for heating and cooking, provide water and transportation, there will be no paying customers and no profits. The public, always ready to criticize big business, crown corporations, and government services would be up in arms.

No one should walk in fear of an earthquake, or always be on the lookout for some place to duck when the earth starts to move, but those who can walk most freely will be those who have accepted responsiblity for their own safety and welfare in the event of a disaster of great magnitude. There are many things that can be done. Architects and engineers say that for starters we must pick our building sites more carefully and design better and stronger. Kobe, Japan, and Los Angeles, California have provided the latest examples of what needs to be done and where the greatest dangers lie. There's also lots of advice available from the utilities for low-cost personal and property protection, but how many have taken the recommendations to heart?

For the past six years or so a core of emergency preparedness people have been putting out messages which are now getting through the wall of apathy. A spate of recent Pacific quakes has reduced criticism about official fear- mongering. More people pay more attention to Emergency Preparedness Week in B.C., basically a time of instruction and publicity.

One group of Fraser Valley school children instead of selling chocolate bars or peanuts to raise funds is offering emergency preparedness kits to the homeowner. This drive by the students of West Langley elementary school was organized by the parent-advisory committee.

In 1995, for the first time, McDonald's was one of the sponsors on the Emergency Preparedness Week publicity poster. If they believe it's worth doing something to prevent the golden arches from falling down in the event of a McQuake, so they can flip and serve billions more hamburgers, it's a good lead for all, including the tofu crowd.

GREATEST KILLER QUAKES

Year	Location	Magnitude	No. Killed
1927	China	8.3	200,000
1920	China	8.6	100,000
1923	Japan	8.3	100,000
1990	Iran	7.7	50,000
1939	Chile	8.3	28,000
1978	Iran	7.7	25,000
1988	Armenia	6.9	25,000
1976	Guatamala	7.5	22,800
1985	Mexico	8.1	9,500
1995	Japan	6.8	6,000
1960	Chile	9.5	5,000
1980	Italy	7.2	4,800
1980	Algeria	7.3	4,500

Source - Associated Press

Kobe: Parts of the elevated railway were destroyed

FOR WHOM THE BELL TOLLS

What is an earthquake? Geofacts, a publication of the Geological Survey of Canada, describes it as the rapid shaking of the earth's surface - sometimes violent - that follows the sudden release of energy from within the earth. The energy release can be created by a sudden fracture between large blocks of material, a volcanic eruption or the movement of molten material at depth. Most earthquakes are caused by sudden breaks in the upper layers of the earth's crust. (For terminology see Appendix A, p. 151)

Scientists know what causes earthquakes even if they can't predict precisely when they will occur. Intense heat from the earth's molten middle produces convection currents which rise toward the crust of our still-cooling planet. This crust is broken into continent-sized sections called plates which form the land masses and the ocean floors. There are four plates off the Pacific Coast of North America, under the ocean, and all are moving, ever so slowly, forced in one direction or another by currents rising from the earth's centre. Over long periods pressure builds up where the plates meet and one tries to force its way under or over another. This pressure must be released and so tremors occur along the edges of the plates, new fractures appear in the earth's surface, volcanos erupt, and lava flows down mountainsides. Then the inner earth is quiet again for a while.

One of the Earth's particularly active earthquake zones circles the Pacific Ocean and is known as the "Ring of Fire." It runs along the coast of Asia, north to the Aleutians and Alaska and then south along the coast of North and South America. B.C. is the most active earthquake zone in Canada, the St. Lawrence Valley is second.

Dr. Dieter Weichert has spent nearly a lifetime on the study of the inner earth. He and his colleagues at the Pacific Geoscience Centre approach the complexities and mysteries of earth science with fascination and enthusiasm.

Explaining the workings of inner earth and the damage inflicted by earthquakes in as simple a way as possible, Dr. Weichert said: "Small earthquakes have their strongest energy in short period waves, big earthquakes in longer-period waves." They compare to the sound waves produced by the ringing of small and big bells. Both types can be devastating. The amount of damage depends on where they are centred, whether they affect inhabited or uninhabited areas, and whether the regions are under the sea, in the mountains or on valley floors.

Huge quakes have occured in the past off the coast of southwestern B.C. and knowledge of them is only now coming to light. Smaller ones occur constantly and if you live in Vancouver's Lower Mainland or on Vancouver Island, you're in a hotbed of activity. You may be one of those for whom the bell tolls soon.

Some scientists are convinced that one of the rare, big, subduction quakes will come again to the Pacific Northwest although there are a few dissenting voices. According to one recent scientific paper on the subject, the Cascadia Subduction Zone stretching along the Oregon, Washington, B.C. coast as far as northern Vancouver Island, could produce a quake that would cause a several hundred kilometres long rupture in the earth's surface. The resulting massive release of energy would be centred deep within the earth at the juncture of the North American plate with the small plates which sit off the coast. In 1993, scientists established that Vancouver Island was tipping to the east. They believe this is part of the buildup that will lead to this giant subduction earthquake centred offshore, beneath the continental shelf. It's likely to arrive within the next 300 years. The Juan de Fuca and Explorer plates which lie offshore are constantly pushing to the northeast, forcing their way under The North American Plate. These colliding plates can produce two types of earthquakes either of which would provide an earth shattering experience for all of us.

Over long periods of time the earth is subjected to stresses and distortions that cause mountains to rise and continents to drift apart. Earthquakes large and small help to release the stress which builds constantly throughout the "Ring of Fire". Also part of this firey halo are the volcanos of the

Garibaldi and Cascade mountain ranges stretching for 1,000 kilometres from B.C. into northern California. At the northern end of the chain is Mount Garibaldi, which has not had a major eruption for about 10,000 years, and Mount Meager, which erupted some 2,400 years ago with a huge explosion that dumped volcanic ash as far away as southern Alberta. In Washington State are Mount Baker, Mount Rainier, and the infamous Mount St. Helens that blew its top in 1980.

Earthquakes are centred either in the crust of the North American plate, within the oceanic plates, or on the boundary where the plates collide. About 90-percent of the hundreds of small quakes which occur regularly are sub-crustal, located within the continental crust. In B.C. most are centred about 20 kilometres below the surface, generally deeper than California quakes which occur at a depth of only 10 kilometres. Because of this there are fewer aftershocks in B.C. although a subset of ongoing, small earthquakes does occur in the upper 10 kilometres and these have a long aftershock sequence, tiny tremors you seldom feel.

Vancouver lies at the northern end of an area of earthquake activity that extends to the south end of Puget Sound in Washington State. Here sub-crustal earthquakes occur in the descending, oceanic Juan de Fuca plate as it moves under the North American plate. These are restricted to about magnitude seven because the young subducting plate is thin, less than 20 kilometres thick, and probably produces rupture lengths of less than 100 kilometres. Rarely have aftershocks been produced by these quakes beneath Vancouver Island, in the Straight of Georgia or in Puget Sound.

The notorious San Andreas fault which runs for 1,200 kilometres across California and out into the Pacific is the centre of many earthquakes which arise from a sideways slipping sub-crustal motion. The Queen Charlotte fault some 600 kilometres north of Vancouver is the centre of a similar sideways slipping motion. Both of these faults are too far away to have an effect on Vancouver or Victoria, but in 1949, the Queen Charlotte fault produced Canada's largest recorded quake, an 8.1.

FOR WHOM THE BELL TOLLS

Intensive recent study of coastal areas in the Cascadia region has provided geologists with evidence that indicates a giant subduction earthquake has occured in the past every 300 to 800 years. This was determined by analysing sand and rock samples and was confirmed by the meticulous records about "tsunamis" or tidal waves maintained by the Japanese. Their observations aided greatly in making the calculations that pinpointed the date of the last catastrophic quake off the B.C. coast, 300 years ago. It occured at 9 p.m. on January 26 in the year 1700. The resulting tsunami was about two metres high when it hit Japan. While there were few people in the Canadian west to record the devastation, there is a legend that tells of a huge wave which struck coastal villages in the darkness, in the depth of winter and everything was gone.

Dr. William Bakun, a seismologist at the U.S. Geological Survey in California, has pointed out that a Cascadia subduction quake along the coast of Washington and B.C. could be as big as anything so far recorded with modern equipment.

It is frightening to imagine the consequences. The Alaska quake of 1964 was a subduction quake and the most devastating to be recorded on the west coast of North America. Pictures of the upheaval show a land torn apart. They are hard to believe. A subduction quake affecting B.C. would be located about 150 kilometres west of Vancouver in the Pacific Ocean where the Juan de Fuca and North American plates are locked in conflict. When next one of them gives way, a tsunami will head for Japan and the west coast of Vancouver Island and the Queen Charlottes will be inundated. Rivers and low lands on the west coast will be flooded. Victoria's harbour could suffer the results of a damaging wave. Near Vancouver the low-lying International Airport and parts of Delta and Richmond could expect several centimetres of salt water on the land although the west coast of the Island would take the brunt of the wave
.

The Lower Mainland and Vancouver Island could be damaged at any time by this subduction quake or by a crustal quake. In 1946, B.C.'s most damaging quake was centred near Courtenay on Vancouver Island and had a magnitude of 7.3. The crustal tremor lasted only 20 or 30 seconds and created minor damage throughout the Island and as far away as Vancouver. Recent quakes which devastated Kobe and Los Angeles occured in heavily populated areas and were characterized as intra-plate or crustal earthquakes. Their destructive force, even though they were short-lived, was awesome because they were centred fairly close to the surface. In Kobe, more than 6,000 people died and there was a crippling financial cost for the country.

Although sometimes less devastating and slightly more predictable because they give advance warning of an eruption are the world's active volcanos. In the Cascades is the highly visible and most active, Mt. St. Helen's, which exploded in 1980 with a force of 24-megatons after a period of relative quiet which had lasted for 123 years. St. Helen's first gave warning something was about to happen on March 27 that year when a series of small earthquakes opened a small crater near the summit. This was followed by jets of ash and steam. Below the new crater the mountain began to bulge as magma welled up from deep within the earth.

Seven-and-a-half weeks later following 10,000 more recorded tremors, the bulge erupted at 8:32 a.m. on May 18 with a magnitude of 5.1 on the Richter scale. The whole upper north flank of the mountain collapsed devastating an area of 600 square kilometres. Rock, mud, water, trees and everything that had been there exploded outward producing the largest landslide in the recorded history of the Pacific northwest. Moving at 1,000 kilometres an hour, the lateral blast levelled 60,000 hectares of forest, killed 57 people who failed to get out of its way, about 5,000 deer, 1,500 elk and 200 bears as well as thousands of fish and birds. Ash and smoke drifted as far as Saskatchewan and people in B.C., Alberta, Washington and Oregon could smell sulphur in the air. The peak of Mt. St. Helen's, an almost perfect cone which had often been compared to Mount Fuji in Japan, was gone and in its place was a lopsided crater rimmed by jagged rock.

Mt. Baker, which is so clearly visible from the Fraser Valley, is still cooling from a minor eruption in 1870. In May, 1995, a U.S. seismologist reported that Mr. Rainier had the highest potential in the Cascades for land-slides because of its steep slopes and continuing seismic activity.

Dr. Weichert and his colleagues watch the world and all its underground activity from an idyllic place, the North Saanich Geoscience Centre directly across the peninsula from Sidney, established by the Federal government in 1978. Shared with the fisheries department, it contains sophisticated listening and measuring equipment that tracks earth tremors and disturbances around the world.

Pinned on the wall outside Dr. Weichert's office was a piece of paper with all the up-and-down squiggles that seismographs record when the earth moves. It stated simply:

Teleseismic	Distant earthquake
Time	12.46 PST
Date	17 January, 1995
Magnitude	6.8
Location	near Kobe, Japan
	latitude 34.67 north
	longitude 135.04 east

Many casualties, severe damage, fires, liquefaction

That, in a nutshell, was the quake that killed thousands, many of them elderly living in old houses whose collapse was partly due to the weight of old-fashioned Japanese roof tiles, and caused enough financial loss from industry shut-downs and collapsed premises to disrupt world markets as money was brought home from overseas to help pay the bills.

Even in quake-conscious Japan, this was a surprise. Experts believed that the biggest threat to Kobe, a port like Vancouver with surrounding mountains, was from a subduction fault some 200 kilometres out to sea. What they got was a shallow intra-plate quake almost directly under the city.

FOR WHOM THE BELL TOLLS

In Kobe many houses collapsed under the weight of heavy, old-fashioned, roof tiles

The same scenario could occur in Vancouver. In the last big shock in California, a territory which is probably the most seismically scrutinized in the world, the Northridge shake in 1994 came from a fault no one knew existed. Apart from being surprised, these communities had one fortunate thing in common, both quakes came in the early morning before rush hour. Thousands more would have been killed if it had been later in the day when bridges and overpasses collapsed and parts of Kobe's elevated railway system fell.

These are the variables and unknowns that Dr. Weichert and his colleagues must deal with in their continuing search for the secrets of the good earth and the prediction of earthquakes to come. In April, 1996, there was a suggestion that scientists may soon be better able to predict an earthquake. A respected authority in the U.S. successfully predicted four moderate earthquakes on the San Andreas fault. He is Clifford Thurber, from the University of Wisconsin, who tracked movements known as "creep events" along this fault and said they gave him up to five days notice of an earthquake.

Seismographs at the Pacific Geoscience centre record some 200 quakes a year in southwest B.C., almost all of them too slight to be felt. Measuring a quake is also a changing science. The Richter scale has been in use for many years. A two on the scale is seldom noticed unless it is "directly under foot" but a seven would bring devastation if it occured close to any heavily populated area. On Richter's scale an increase of one number represents an amplification 10 times greater than the previous number. An increase of two numbers represents an amplification of 100. Move up to the sevens and beyond and there's a whole lot of shaking going on.

Dr. Weichert explains that scientists today prefer another means of calculating quakes which they believe is more precise. It's called the Moment Magnitude Scale and measures the total "moment" or "momentum" of the quake, a concept similar to energy release. One can be a long way from the epicentre of a quake but still be greatly affected by movement along a fault more than a hundred kilometres long.

Scientists say a quake can make the surface shake, sink or slide and maybe do all three. The shaking is a resonance which occurs at the epicentre and sharply amplifies the intensity of the shockwaves. Liquefaction is just

Bridges and overpasses collapsed and parts of Kobe's elevated railway system fell

what the word implies. The earth's tremors turn soil and moisture into a sticky, gooey mess on which buildings slide, slip off their foundations or perhaps tilt and fall when the ground beneath them becomes liquid.

University of B. C. scientists suggest liquefaction could occur extensively in the municipalities of Delta and Richmond and in other communities along river banks and flat lands. As occured in Kobe, the land could drop a third of a metre more or less, resulting in structural damage and flooding. When houses are not well secured to their foundations, they can "take a walk" as one engineer put it.

Rock slides are common both during or following an earthquake. Often huge rock faces break free and come roaring down mountains. This could happen in the north shore mountains of Vancouver or along Highway 99 from Horseshoe Bay to Squamish, a stretch of highway which frequently experiences rain-induced slides. "Rolling rock" and washouts are a way of life for people who travel this route on a regular basis. It has been suggested that at least one recent slide along this road to the Whistler ski area was triggered by a minor quake. Some scientists disagree.

When Canada extended its national jurisdiction 200 miles offshore in 1977, there was a renewed effort to find out exactly what lies beneath the ocean and this became a prime function of the Geoscience Centre. It is perhaps fortunate that Canada wanted to stake its claim to the treasures beneath the sea because in the process it has become much more knowledgeable about the whole subject of subduction earthquakes. Modern equipment is used in the sea quest including underwater cameras and a deep-diving submersible. Both Canada's Pisces IV and the U.S. Alvin have been down filming and probing along the Juan de Fuca Ridge, seeking data on plate movement. At the same time they sample hydrothermal minerals deposited there by undersea volcanos in the hope that at some future time they will have an economic value. Dr. Weichert and his colleagues also are aided today by space science and information relayed from satellites that have instruments observing earth's movement.

Of immediate importance is the work done in connection with the National Building Code. In 1995, Dr. Weichert and three colleagues presented a paper which refined the seismic maps of the Lower Mainland. These show the status of various areas and how they might fare in a quake. This information plays a part in siting, planning and identifying the preferred types of construction. It is expected that the findings in the latest maps which take into account the possibility of a subduction quake off the west coast with a magnitude of eight or more will lead to revisions in the building code scheduled for the year 2000.

ARE YOU COVERED?

If the insurance industry trembles a little at the thought of a major earthquake hitting the Lower Mainland, its discomfort is understandable. There just isn't the money to pay recovery costs after a major episode and it's doubtful if there could ever be enough. This doesn't mean that the 30-odd percent of B.C. householders who currently have taken out policies should say "Well, what the hell ...." and rip them up. The industry can take care of shingle shakers, minor quakes and localized tremors but in the event of a major one in the Vancouver area, it can't pay the bill.

At a Canadian insurance congress held in Vancouver in April, 1995, John Thompson, Federal Deputy Superintendent of Financial Institutions, said that a major earthquake in Vancouver threatens the very survival of the property and casualty insurance industry in Canada. In reality the threat goes far beyond the insurance industry.

"This is a national problem", he said. "If there is a major earthquake in the Lower Mainland today, some of the residents of Ontario will be breaking the law by driving their automobiles because they will not be insured. If a company is hit by heavy losses from earthquake claims arising from a natural event in the Vancouver area, it could be out of business in all lines in all jurisdictions."

Thompson also pointed out that a major earthquake could have devastating implications for mortgage lenders, including banks, trust companies and credit unions. "They don't always insist that borrowers have adequate earthquake insurance. If that's the case and a major earthquake occurs involving properties in their mortgage portfolio, the security behind those mortgages could be of little value," he said.

With a possible financial future of total bankruptcy, the insurance odds-makers have given as much thought as anyone to the problem. A 1992 study by the Munich Reinsurance Company of Canada looked at the economic consequences of what could happen in the Lower Mainland. The study was the most comprehensive ever done on this question and remains the bible when potential cost is being assessed. The findings were widely quoted in a paper produced in the fall of 1994 by the Insurance Bureau of Canada, the private general insurers' association and lobby group. While couched in the most cautious, insurance-industry language, the paper urged with justification that it was time governments as well as the business and commercial world took a look at where they stand. In fact, negotiations between the insurance industry, the B.C. and federal governments are on-going in an attempt to rewrite laws and regulations and to resolve an issue which could threaten the economic stability of the whole country.

Just one of the problems is an obvious concern. If your house suffers earthquake damage and you don't have specific insurance, too bad. However, if your house then catches fire, your normal B.C. fire insurance kicks in. In pragmatic Quebec it's different. Once the shaking starts, your fire insurance is automatically cancelled. Quebec doesn't mind if people call on divine help in such trouble, but it doesn't want any other possible calls for do-it-yourself fires.

The insurance industry has proposed a four-part solution to reduce the financial impact of a major earthquake. It wants insurance companies themselves to improve their risk management, to tighten discipline, to promote activities that reduce the amount of property damage and loss, such as seismic upgrading, and to create a pre-funded reserve to ensure claims other than those incurred by a major disaster can be met. Even with industry-wide perseverance there would be a shortfall. At the April '95 meeting, one insurer told the assembly that B.C. residents were insured for about $10 billion worth of property damage but the industry might only be able to cover $2.6 billion.

A major split within the industry is the dogfight for business. In the IBC paper headed "Industry Discipline", the following words indicate there isn't much of it as companies pursue the mighty dollar: "Despite the efforts of some companies to employ current technology in evaluating their exposures (obscure talk for how big a financial bath they could take) and to provide appropriate levels of protection, other companies continue to operate on short time horizons which completely discount the real threat of earthquake losses in B.C. and Quebec. As long as some companies are allowed to discount earthquake risk to the point of negating it in their pricing decisions, companies who more accurately reflect the risk in their marketing decisions are placed at a competitive disadvantage."

The study by the Munich group spells out how devastating a quake could be. Hopes, dreams and aspirations of thousands of people would be wiped out in seconds. They could face years of picking up the pieces and starting over again, providing they were among the lucky ones who survived.

A major quake has implications that go far beyond the Lower Mainland. Reduce thousands of B.C. workers from taxpayers to aid recipients and the national coffers take a tremendous beating. The implications are much greater for Canada and its population of 30 million than a similar disaster would mean in the U.S. or Japan with more people and bigger economies.

Apart from stating that the older part of Vancouver, Gastown and the east end with its old brick buildings, would come down like a pack of cards along with a lot of homes, commercial buildings, bridges and other structures built more than 25 years ago, the Munich study looked into other aspects of the economy, including such things as the amount of travel time that would be lost because of downed or damaged bridges, ripped up highways and streets.

An earthquake measuring 6.5 on the Richter scale in southwestern B.C. was used as a base for the Munich study, and, of course, things would be a whole lot worse in a larger shake. This was the assessment:"...the loss of 20 percent of all buildings in the GVRD - the equivalent of the complete decimation of all residences in the City of Vancouver, or the destruction of all commercial and institutional buildings in the municipalities of North Vancouver City, North Vancouver District, Port Coquitlam, Port Moody, Richmond, Surrey, Vancouver and West Vancouver."

ARE YOU COVERED?

So much for real estate values.

The IBC report adds: "Other estimates from the same study predict the loss of up to $100 million worth of bridges, $200 million worth of roads and a further $200 million in sewage treatment infrastructure." Totalling up the tab, the report concludes that the economic cost of a quake of the selected magnitude in a large urban centre could "range from $15 to $32 billion. Thirty billion in damaged buildings and failed infrastructure represents one-third of the province's annual gross domestic product and an economic shock ten times greater than the most recent recession." Hit the area with a 7.5 on the Richter Scale, 10 times stronger than the study envisioned, and you can make your own guess as to the cost. It would be catastrophic. The Bureau's heading for this section reads, truthfully enough, "There is a Problem - Damage We Can't Pay For."

The industry suggests that if all the knowledge gained in recent years in technology, social research and public policy related to loss mitigation (the popular word in the business for taking measures to cut losses ahead of the event) produced some action, Greater Vancouver would be in much better shape to face a quake. The report says municipal officials should take their courage in their hands, take a long-term perspective and act for the future by passing laws and spending money on matters that their more optimistic, laid-back taxpayers might not immediately appreciate.

Current Canadian policy towards earthquakes involves three activities: emergency preparedness, loss mitigation and compensation, and recognizing that the individual has primary responsibility for his or her own skin. The federal and provincial governments both have emergency plans in place and have practiced procedures. One exercise in the fall of 1995 involved 21 provincial departments and various organizations, but no one has gone into the long-term problems of how B.C. might start to meet the tremendous cost of a quake or the source of funds for recovery. It would go far beyond provincial resources and a cash-strapped federal government would also have problems.

ARE YOU COVERED?

The force of a quake can be truly awesome. The 1994 Northridge shake in California produced the second most expensive natural disaster in the U.S. in recent years, exceeded only by Hurricane Andrew.

To quote the IBC report: "In British Columbia, while all buildings constructed since 1985 have generally been designed to withstand tremendous shaking brought on by a sizeable earthquake, only an estimated 50-percent of buildings constructed between 1960 and 1985 were designed to survive an earthquake and buildings erected before 1941 for the most part have no built-in earthquake tolerance."

Note the use of the words "sizeable" and "generally". Even if your building was built since 1985, don't count on too much.

The biggest problem states the report is buildings made of masonry or concrete with no or improper reinforcement to resist sideways movement. Even in earthquake-conscious California, where the building regulations are tougher, all kinds of problems have been identified in steel-and-concrete highrises. Most of them occur where beams and girders are joined by bolts and welding. In many cases in recent quakes these have been found deficient. To fix one can cost from $5,000 to $50,000 and there could be a thousand such joins in a large building. Try adding that up. Most modern highrises can withstand considerable swaying caused by tremors, they're built so that the tremors abate as they go up the building. Low-rise concrete buildings may fare badly as tremors travel a shorter distance at full velocity. Although it is unlikely, a building could also sustain a form of whiplash. This can occur when the first tremor starts the building swaying from left to right, and a second tremor moves in the opposite direction. A building has not yet been snapped in two so far as anyone knows, but it's possible.

IBC points out that as much as half of the economic loss following a quake would be from fire, and the National Fire Safety Code does not have any special provisions for areas such as the Lower Mainland which would be

ARE YOU COVERED?

ripe for roaring blazes. At Kobe, 16 hours after the 1995 shock, some 75,000 square metres of the city were ablaze.

After noting construction and fire problems and the need for the public to be better able to look after itself, the report found: "Building standards for new construction fail to address the larger issue of the failure of the current building stock....Municipal bylaws concerning seismic upgrading during change of use have not been highly successful — the municipal bylaw concerning seismic retrofitting in the Greater Vancouver area has led to only 500 improved structures in the 20 years since its implementation....Funding for mitigation activities in the broader, public sector remains inadequate — the Vancouver School Board has only managed to finance the seismic upgrade of two of the more than 50 schools which are inadequately constructed to protect the city's children."

Low-rise concrete buildings may fare badly

Community representatives all indicated concern about their school properties. The provincial government, however, imposed a moratorium in 1994 on further funding for upgrading pending additional study. Lack of funds and the high cost of this work is the stumbling block.

Vancouver has the greatest number of older schools, with more than 300 buildings in 109 locations. To upgrade the worst conditions in two schools and to secure funds for another two, amounted to an expenditure of close

Are You Covered?

to $20 million. Some $6 million was spent on Sir Charles Tupper Secondary and $4.6 million on Britannia Secondary, part of which was built in
1913. The two elementary schools are Selkirk and McBride for which $4
million each was approved prior to the moratorium but the money had not
been released by the early summer of 1996.

The Insurance Bureau report notes that individuals are unlikely to take
steps to look after themselves and their property without incentives. Looking at compensation, the problem is the premise that the individual has the
initial responsibility in insurance. It states: "In practice the current Canadian earthquake insurance market fails in both its ability to encourage loss-
mitigative activity, and in its ability to equitably and fully compensate those
suffering losses. Both the institutional context for earthquake insurance in
Canada and the behavior within the insurance market itself contribute to
this outcome."

The question of fire insurance is a major burner. The report states:..."There
are currently two types of insurance protection for losses from a major
earthquake: earthquake shaking protection (typically purchased by endorse-
ment) and earthquake fire protection (covered under the basic habitational
and commerical policies). In general, these policies/endorsements are subject to different terms and conditions which have the effect of providing
more generous compensation to policy holders suffering earthquake fire-
related damage than to the insured suffering earthquake shaking damage.
"This creates a moral hazard for victims of the next earthquake and will
lead to unfair results. Under the current institutional arrangement for providing earthquake insurance it is possible for two households facing similar dollar amounts of damage from the same catastrophic event to face
significantly different levels of support from their insurance company.
Suppose one household took the precaution of stabilizing appliances, while
the other did not — should this household which perhaps averted fire damage as a result receive less compensation than his neighbour?" Indeed, a
moral hazard problem — the complexities of the situation have resulted in
a cry from the Bureau that something be done quickly through a combined

effort by the government, the industry and all concerned to iron it out. The report adds that actions by some companies to raise deductibles or write new restrictions are not viable long term solutions.

The industry's estimated probable maximum loss for personal and commercial property exposures in B.C. was $9.7 billion, under current purchase patterns. The research estimated the financial impact of losses of this magnitude would mean that the industry's capacity to pay (defined as reinsurance, plus a proxy for industry retention) was an estimated $2.3 billion in B.C. and "falls short of being able to meet earthquake claim demands." The shortfall appears to be huge.

The industry, naturally, stressed the need for insurance as a key component to the country's response to earthquake havoc. It pointed out, for example, that coverage and premiums keyed to the amount of loss-reduction measures taken by individual owners in their own protection would be an important move.

"Governments, property and casualty insurers and others should begin work immediately to evaluate the regulatory rules and industry practices which have enabled the industry to enter this solvency crisis," stated the report, having earlier noted that the undisciplined fight among companies for the dollar was a key cause of the problem.

The Bureau added: "These same groups should also study the reasons why many Canadians who are knowingly at risk do not voluntarily purchase earthquake insurance or take other mitigative measures, and consider alternatives for ensuring the fulfilment of society's needs to reduce earthquake exposure and meet the next earthquake's reconstruction costs."
The Bureau also makes a call for muscle. It urges tougher building codes and..."innovative ways to ensure compliance with and enforcement of the codes."

Former Provincial Finance Minister Elizabeth Cull gave the industry part of the answer during a meeting in Vancouver in 1995 where she said: "We want to establish a standard for assessing the adequacy of each insurer's earthquake capacity." She also indicated building codes will be amended to ensure new structures are more able to withstand earthquakes and private insurers will be encouraged to use new technology to measure their financial exposure to earthquakes more accurately.

While Cull indicated she was not in a hurry to establish some kind of a special earthquake fund she did suggest: "We need to find ways to deal with the lack of capacity to pay out in face of a possible major quake through a provincial reinsurance plan which will generate sufficient accumulated premiums to safeguard against a future disaster. Even putting aside the private loss, the public loss would be staggering so we have to do what we can to mitigate against that loss."

While IBC is basically concerned with looking after itself, its financial liability and its shareholders, the entire earthquake picture is murky. Just as everyone wants to go to heaven but no one wants to die, all parties from governments to individuals would like to be better protected without it costing anything. This can't be done. It's also difficult to convince the public that its much better to dig deeper in your pocket than to dig your grave.

In its assessment of the economic loss to the Lower Mainland, the Munich company made some intriguing discoveries as it sought to find some reasonable conclusions. It was an incredibly difficult study. Based on its 6.5 Richter scale model, the estimates of damage ranged up to $32 billion and beyond. There are so many variables in quakes that it is daunting to venture into this area of prediction. At least it was a start and the first real examination of what the future might hold.

Many older buildings collapsed or suffered severe damage

Some 6,300 people died and large portions of a mountain ringed port city were shattered and set ablaze in the earthquake that rocked Kobe, Japan, January 17, 1995. Unlike the quakes in California, when Canadians sat for hours glued to live TV coverage of the carnage, in one instance even watching the tremors occur, coverage of Kobe was after the event and shorter term. Although far removed from Vancouver, it was the most damaging Pacific Rim quake in recent years and one from which much can be learned. This is how a B.C. team of scientists and engineers found the scene shortly after the disaster.

The 6.8 magnitude quake in Kobe produced not only devastation for the city but major problems for the Japanese economy. Kobe has three-percent of the Japanese population and five-percent of the country's gross national product (GNP). Japan had to pull back some of its overseas money to help pay the huge cost of recovery. Should an earthquake devastate the Lower Mainland, its impact on the Canadian economy would be much greater than Kobe's was on Japan, despite the importance of that city's terminals. The Port of Vancouver is one of the top three in North America and in 1995 its throughput totalled 71.5 million tonnes. Collapse of the Lions Gate Bridge is a possibility and this would effectively close the port to all shipping.

The Kobe quake occured just before 6 a.m. and by 10 p.m. there were 75,000 square metres of the city on fire. More than 23,000 homes burned and in excess of 2,000 ruptured water lines made fire fighting all but impossible. Buildings came down and rubble clogged the narrow streets. All transit systems failed and the main highway was down to one lane from six. Sections of the city's grain terminals collapsed along with their conveyor systems. Pilings were fractured. Soya and oil storage facilities were hard hit and piping was misaligned. There was total failure or severage damage to most of the tall concrete smoke stacks. Cast iron piping connections installed in the 1950s and 60s snapped. Many older buildings collapsed or suffered severe damage. Major industries were badly damaged, some of them knocked out for lengthy periods.

The city's bridges took a beating, even the new ones. The new hospital's walls remained standing, but operating rooms and other essential facilities were useless because ceilings and poorly installed overhead fixtures came crashing down, filling rooms with debris. The water system failed and it was a bucket brigade of volunteers who came to the rescue by carrying water from a ship in the harbor to the partly-functioning hospital. Communications were chaotic because of over centralization and the collapse of a main tower.

Kobe found that its earthquake preparedness was not as good as officials believed it to be and blame was handed out during inquiries that followed the disaster.

When a major quake strikes anywhere in the world, the U.S. bankrolls a team to get to the scene to learn as much as it can in their own interest. In Canada it's more of a pass-the-hat operation. The Canadian Association for Earthquake Engineering (CAEE) doesn't have ready access to federal money, but it did send a team to Kobe. There was partial federal financing, some companies helped, and one airline kicked in some tickets. The team was organized by Dr. Sheldon Cherry, of the University of B.C., the then president of CAEE. The current president is Dr. Art Heidericht, of McMaster University, Hamilton.

Dr. Cherry said that in the 1960s the National Research Council formed a national committee for earthquake engineering. In the early 1990s the NRC restructured the committee and gave it a singularly focused mandate as an independent body. The group currently has about 200 members across Canada, mainly engineers, geologists, and seismologists but the organization is open to other interested individuals such as planners, architects, social scientists, and public officials. There is a time for detailed study of reports made following such disasters. There is also a need to be on the scene as soon as possible in order to gain a full appreciation of the devastation and provide an opportunity for examination of the type of damage and the immediate and long-term effects on the community. That's why the

DEADLY LESSONS FROM KOBE

CAEE group went to Kobe.

There are some obvious comparisons between Vancouver and the Japanese city, a port backed by mountains and with much of the waterfront built on landfill, including two man-made islands. Despite the intensity of the quake and considerable liquefaction, the more modern buildings in Kobe held up well. Many of the problems confronted by the Japanese could be expected if a similar quake hit the Lower Mainland.

After his trip to the Far East, UBC's Dr. Peter Byrne, revised some of his earlier thinking about the possible affects of a quake on the Fraser River delta. It could be less than he had thought, but a massive disaster nevertheless. "In Richmond and Delta the earth could drop a third of a metre or more which would create terrible problems for all services, from water to transit," said Dr. Byrne. "Dikes would be breached and there would be widespread flooding."

Liquefaction would cause problems for many buildings in the area, but those built more recently and to code — and much of the area is new residential and commercial accommodation — could withstand shaking without collapsing. There would be widespread damage, however, and equipment not securely bolted down could fall over. Byrne says liquefaction likely would damage roads leading to the Tsawwassen ferry dock and rail lines going to the Roberts Bank bulk loading terminal.

He sees many of the bridges in the Lower Mainland as major problems. It is ironic that in at least two cases, one end of a bridge sits on fill while the other end is reasonably secure: the Stanley Park end of Lions Gate is on rock, but the north end is on fill. Similarly, while the south end of the Oak Street Bridge sits on liquefaction-prone land in Richmond, the north end is more secure in Marpole. Any sandy soil or fill at water level that has not been well compacted before construction will not support a large structure during a quake.

In Kobe, where some of the older spans fell, the problem in newer bridges came from the failure of large ball-bearings which had been installed to permit horizontal and vertical movement in the bridge supports. As a result most of the bridges were knocked out of action.

Failure of large ball-bearings caused the collapse of even some of the newer bridges

Byrne's observations on the George Massey Tunnel lend weight to the opinions of many engineers who feel that bumper-to-bumper under the Fraser River isn't where they would want to be during an earthquake. Without predicting a total collapse, Byrne explains that there would be problems at the joints in the tunnel which was built in 100-metre-concrete sections. Some 30 years ago, a trench was dug in the river bottom and the sections were dropped into place. Engineers agree that there's no chance this would be the construction method chosen if the tunnel were built today.

Dr. Byrne is no great fan of Japanese construction, noting wryly that their large concrete structures are not nearly as good as their cars, television sets or watches. Kobe was extremely fortunate that it wasn't rush hour when long lengths of the elevated railway fell to the ground.

He comments that Vancouver could be in an earthquake lull: "While we're in a quiet period right now, pressure and movement could be building and an intra-plate quake could be much worse for Vancouver than a subduction one."

Also in Kobe was Dr. John Sherstobitoff, the principal seismic engineer with Sandwell Inc., who has been on the spot following several major quakes. He said the American funding system that permits a team to move quickly to a disaster provides an opportunity for a first-hand look at how things are working.

Sherstobitoff said that in Kobe newer buildings constructed to recent building codes held up even if cladding fell off the outside walls and ceilings were damaged or fell inside. Surprisingly, although tall buildings swayed, there was not much glass breakage.

The engineer said that about five-percent more spending on a building to exceed minimum requirements of the Canadian building code is money well spent to obtain a building that will suffer significantly less damage in a major earthquake. Additional expenditures on better restraint of electrical wiring, heating ducts and water pipes is also good value. Ruptured sprinkler systems caused serious damage in many Kobe buildings that had no fires.

Sherstobitoff said that the Kobe experience shows it is essential that more attention be paid to strengthening schools, especially gymnasiums where the homeless are often housed. Some work has been done in the Lower Mainland, but more is needed, and the sooner, the better.

The engineer added that a population with some knowledge and training in emergency preparedness is invaluable. "We should all be on a rapid learning curve."

Sherstobitoff pointed to one deficiency that bothers him personally. After a quake engineers are desperately needed to assess which damaged buildings are beyond hope and should be pulled down, and which ones are safe to enter. A move to coordinate volunteer engineers for the job is in the doldrums here. "I and many others offered our services for this work to several organizations and despite having done so some time ago, I have heard nothing back", he added.

Bill McKevitt, from McKevitt Engineering, also was with the CAEE group. He said communications in the city were badly disrupted when the building holding the main transmission tower was damaged and the system went down. In future the Japanese won't have all their eggs in one basket and a series of satellites will be constructed. He also pointed to problems at Kobe Steel which in addition to structural damage was shut down because of heat, light and air conditioning failures caused by ceiling collapses.

Among McKevitt's other observations was one that strengthens the belief that a tidy desk prevents chaos. People in many companies who left working papers on their desks lost them in the post-quake confusion. Debris from ceilings and light fixtures came crashing down scattering and destroying everything. Wherever working documents were neatly tucked away they provided a head start to the recovery process.

The damaged port scene was surveyed by Jiti Khann of Khann Consultants International. He noted that 65-percent of the infrastructure in the quake area was knocked out of commission and about 90-percent of Kobe's port operation was brought to a shuddering halt. The artificial islands at Kobe are similar to the coal terminal at Roberts Bank near Vancouver and the comparisons are obvious. "We must design port facilities so that they can be fixed quickly," he said.

Slimy fill which boiled up to the surface was one result of liquefaction reported Liam Finn, a geotechnical expert. He said that some piles on the artificial islands settled as much as 20 to 40 centimetres. It is clear, however, that bringing all buildings up to a standard that could survive a major quake would take costs to astronomical levels. Even bringing them up to current standards could only be done at enormous cost, he admitted.

Stores with open fronts tended to collapse

Ron DeVall, of Read, Jones Christoffersen Ltd., who also spoke at a symposium at UBC held after the group's return, said housing constructed to the latest Japanese code fared not too badly. Unfortunately, 90-percent of the dead and injured were the elderly living in old-fashioned homes which collapsed. The weight of heavy ceramic roofing tiles, once popular in Japan, was too much for the older structures to withstand.

DeVall did, however, bring back findings that augur well for the B.C. and Canadian economy. He stated that post-and-beam homes exhibited inconsistent results and stores with open fronts tended to collapse. The dwellings that survived best were those of basic two by four wooden construction, good news for the Canadian forest industry. Much has been done to bring the city of Kobe back from its 20 seconds of destruction which occured on January 17, 1995. Most of the debris has been removed, damaged buildings have been taken down, rail lines have been repaired and trains are running again but many thousands of people remain essentially homeless, living in shelters or make-shift structures. Many families have given up hope of ever owning a home again because they are in debt for the ones they lost. As a result many of the homeless are suffering from serious depression and psychological problems.

Admittedly, Kobe had much to recover from and a final tally of death and destruction shows that as a result of this 20 second 6.8 magnitude shake, 3,266 persons were killed instantly, 1,397 died within six hours and the final toll was more than 6,000 dead and 34,900 injured. Some 250 people perished in fires which erupted after gas lines broke. In the port, 90-percent of the docks were knocked out and eight months later were operating at only 40-percent capacity. Another two years will be required to get things back to normal. Damage is now estimated at the equivalent of $129 billion Canadian and the Japanese have proposed the expenditure of $170 billion more over the next 10 years to develop a "disaster-resistant" metropolis.

Information from the Canadian engineering team that visited Kobe has been disseminated across Canada producing much to think about and learn from, so much so that it would seem a sound investment for government, even in these belt-tightening days, to ensure that a Canadian earthquake investigation team is properly funded. This would ensure speedy despatch to future quakes, something that is very much in our own interest.

When the Line Goes Dead

When the Lower Mainland's rowdies staged their 1994 post-hockey game riot in downtown Vancouver, Burnaby fire crews manned Vancouver fire halls while the city men reported for duty on Robson Street. This was in accordance with a mutual aid agreement but there was a great big hole in the arrangement. Burnaby crews were unable to link up with radio communication at Vancouver dispatch, the "what's-happening" nerve centre of the night. This is typical of the incredible communication chaos in the Greater Vancouver area. In a classic understatement, a recent newspaper article said of the riot snafu - "Fire department staff noted a critical need for communications among fire, ambulance and police."

There is almost a complete lack of compatibility in the communications systems of the 20 municipalities in the GVRD. It's an area of fiercely independent principalities and satraps with a bewildering complexity of services, some focussed firmly on a specific agenda and marching to the beat of their own drums, or in the case of earthquakes, rumbles.

Several recent incidents have left one community totally unable to communicate with another. This has, however, brought a number of organizations together in an effort to do something constructive. An Emergency Operations and Communications Centre (EOCC) is now planned for the Lower Mainland. Some of the participants include: RCMP, Vancouver Fire Dispatch, Vancouver Police Dispatch, GVRDs 911 system and the provincial emergency program. In addition to the EOCC there will be a Regional Emergency Coordination Centre (RECC) at the same location which some municipalities and utilities have agreed to support. There is some disappointment that the list of committed participants is not longer. Workshops were held recently and a 'definition of requirements' for a multi-agency radio system was developed. It is not known where this facility will be located, but it will be a post-earthquake design with adjacent helicopter landing pad.

There is some urgency to move forward with this project as some police and fire departments currently have communications systems - dispatch and 911 - located in older buildings that are among those most likely to come down or be badly damaged in a quake. Vancouver's present Emergency Operations Centre (EOC) is located at the old Police Station on Main street, not a building constructed to current standards nor even those in place during the last 40 years.

Complications have been created by the independent actions of some municipalities to meet their own immediate needs and the study undertaken in preparation for the new facility noted that even implementation of some of these schemes "will significantly impact the possibility of ever achieving an appreciable degree of intermunicipal, inter-agency communication and coordination in the future."

Without integration now of the many existing systems, the cost and efficiency of introducing an overall communications network may forever be out of reach. The $12 to $14 million cost is significant. In 1995 $6 million was obtained through the federal infrastructure program and the study stated: "if additional agencies participate in creating a joint venture, the size and number of participating agencies involved in the project would determine the total cost." The estimate does not include the cost of land.

Some groups appear reluctant participants in the scheme, concerned that smaller operations will be dominated by the thinking of Vancouver. One official said there had been suggestions in the past by other municipalities that there should be coordination, but it had been rejected by Vancouver. In the future, technological improvement in communications will provide something like a super-cellular system that will do away with telephone lines altogether.

It is a paradox that while waiting for some electronic wonder, we come to rely more and more on something from the past — the fairly simple, battery-operated system beloved of ham-radio operators which has proven invaluable in so many disasters. When all the gee-whiz electrical systems have collapsed, hams have kept the links open between devastated com-

When all else fails, ham radios can be relied on to keep the lines of communication open

munities and the outside. Their importance was pointed out as recently as May, 1995, when retired telephone executive Doug Burrows, who lives in Edmonton, helped save three B.C. sailors who were in distress off the U.S. west coast. The 76-year-old operator picked up the SOS and alerted the U.S. Coast Guard which sent a helicopter and rescue cutter to the beleaguered ketch. The importance of this type of transmission is evident at the Emergency Social Services (ESS) communications centre at the Justice Institute of B.C. in New Westminster which relies entirely on the members of the Telephone Pioneers Amateur Radio Club to install and operate its B.C. Digital Emergency Services Network linking all ESS teams during an emergency.

A BATTERY RADIO LIFELINE

If someone had only $20 to spend on earthquake protection how should it be allocated? Without doubt, the first purchase is a battery operated radio and a supply of batteries. In the event that everything else fails, it is certain there will be some form of radio service within a devasted city and information can be picked up from stations operating outside the area. The car radio is an alternative until the battery runs dead, providing it survived the quake.

Greg Barnes, until recently the Canadian Broadcasting Corporation's head of radio services in B.C. and its emergency communications coordinator, had a very large cabinet drawer in his office full of emergency planning documents. He was a member of the Regional Emergency Telecommunications Committee for 12 years and didn't take lightly the corporation's role in an emergency. What concerned him was that in all the years he was involved, "emergency services still hadn't figured out how to get in touch with me." Barnes who has left CBC has been succeeded in the emergency role by regional engineer Ian Munro.

As a government agency, the network has a particular role to play in broadcasting official messages and instructions to the public. With power lines down there is unlikely to be TV and hence the necessity for having a battery radio. CBC headquarters in downtown Vancouver was built to fairly recent building code requirements and is expected to withstand a good shake. It has on-site emergency fuel supplies to keep the network on the air for about four days, but not much longer. There also are self-contained radio vans and other specialized equipment including good old UHF/VHF which Barnes stressed would be a major player in any emergency service. The headquarters has stockpiles of supplies including food, water, bedding and first-aid equipment for staff use.

Recent earthquake disasters made some emergency agencies realize how dependent they would be on broadcasting. Not all reporting is simon pure Barnes admitted, and in the past some officials hesitated to talk to the media about emergency measures. Suspicions have been breaking down though and those involved have now gone to the trouble of training staff in how to make statements and comments on air in a crisis situation. Barnes said there is an Emergency Planners and News Broadcasters Committee that has been meeting for a number of years.

As for commercial radio, John Ashbridge, the operations manager at CKNW, the oldest and most-listened to station with the largest audience in B.C., remembers as a youth in Victoria hearing radio reports coming out of Alaska in 1964 following North America's largest quake this century.

WHEN THE LINE GOES DEAD

He was happy in 1995 when NW moved from an old cinder-block building in New Westminster, a sure-fire loser in a major shake, to the 21st floor of the Toronto Dominion building in downtown Vancouver, a structure that has as good a chance as any of remaining relatively undamaged.

Like CBC, NW has modern equipment including mobile vans. Their main transmitter is on Mt. Seymour and there are backups. Ashbridge says there could be great reliance on UHF/VHF that the station also owns. His advice is the same as others — be smart, have a battery operated set at the office and at home and make sure the batteries work.

Other commercial stations in the Lower Mainland have similar emergency plans and special equipment.

A major effort to inform the public was presented by BCTV in March, and again in June, 1996. Co-produced by Shockwave Productions Inc. and BCTV the graphic one-hour documentary was made to simulate a major provincial-municipal exercise held in the fall of the previous year. The station videod a mock emergency broadcast centre complete with aftershocks, falling ceilings with broadcasters ducking for cover, and reporters in the field interviewing emergency workers. Channel 8 also produced a preparedness brochure for public distribution. (see Appendix B)

GAS — ON OR OFF?

The soil of the Fraser River delta (shaded area) has the potential to amplify ground motion and is suseptible to liquefaction.

GAS — ON OR OFF?

Should you turn off the gas at the metre as soon as the shaking stops? B.C. Gas says, "Not necessarily." This action could, in fact, lead to some very unnecessary misery such as weeks in winter without heat, hot water or fuel for the stove. Company officials say the gas should only be shut off if you smell it, hear it escaping or if structural damage is bad enough to make the whole system suspect.

Gas should be turned on only by a qualified person and relighting thousands and thousands of systems is a mammoth, undertaking. After the Los Angeles quake, 120,000 people turned off the gas when only 15,000 actually needed to do so. The California utility rushed in extra help, but it still took 3,000 workers more than two weeks to turn all the appliances back on and this was a quake over a relatively small area.

This was one of the concerns stressed by Ray Nadeau, Manager for Emergency Planning, and Mike Davies, a project manager with B.C. Gas. A major relighting would be an enormous, time-consuming project because of the large role the utility plays in the everyday life of the province. It has some 700,000 customers — 90-percent of all the people using gas in B.C. — and many residential and commercial customers are located in the Lower Mainland. Gas is cheaper than electricity or oil, and its use is on the increase. There are plentiful supplies in the Peace River districts of B.C. and Alberta, where most of it comes from on a pipeline trip of several hundreds of kilometres over some very rugged country.

The main threat to Lower Mainland supply, however, lies in the relatively short distance between Abbotsford and Vancouver. The problem is the soil of the Fraser River delta, its potential to amplify ground motion during a quake and its susceptibility to liquefaction. Pipelines make various river crossings on bridges that may or may not survive a severe shake and which might shake enough to snap the pipe. The company said studies indicate the lines are fairly secure and measures have been taken to offset the effects of severe vibration. U.S. experts were brought in from California to assess local conditions and a major drilling program will assist in predicting ground movement. Seismic activity in California and around the Pacific Rim, in addition to constant although unfelt miniquakes that always affect B.C., have been a "quake-up call" for this company and other utilities.

B.C. Gas is planning a major operations centre at Lochburn and Boundary in Burnaby to be built to specifications that exceed the present building code. This is where emergency operating decisions will be made on such moves as major shutdowns if pipe is ruptured coming into the Lower Mainland. The utility is more fortunate than its Kobe counterpart because in recent years old, cast-iron pipe has been replaced with new, stronger, more pliable steel or plastic. A modern system to replace the existing low-pressure one is also being installed. This upgrading makes the B.C. Gas system considerably safer than it was a few years ago. Following the Los Angeles quake, where much of the pipe was fairly old, there were 1,400 distribution line breaks.

B.C. Gas has 1,600 employees and 1996 was the year targetted for completion of a new emergency corporate plan. This is an update of a plan which is tested every year as well as during periodic province-wide exercises. Nadeau explained that planning is done at the local level, each department having responsibility for its own part of the master plan which dovetails into the overall corporate scheme. All B.C. Gas employees have received earthquake training and the company also provides information to help employees prepare their homes and neighbourhoods for a major disaster. Like the other major utilities, which know that fast recovery is their economic salvation, B.C. Gas has its own modern communications system ranging from UHF to microwave. It also has specially equipped vehicles to send to the most badly-damaged areas as mobile operation centres.

Knowing that customers can do a lot to help themselves pre-emptively, the utility is working with specialists at the University of B.C. to test methods for securing hot water tanks and other equipment to prevent them from toppling. High-standing tanks which survive intact can provide a safe water

GAS — ON OR OFF?

supply for a family which may be isolated and on its own.

B.C. Gas has produced pamphlets and other public information about earthquakes and the gas supply, even a fridge magnet to explain gas shutoff. The company plans increased participation at home shows and similar exhibitions on self-protection. Company President Stephen Bellringer is chairman of the Emergency Preparation Industry Council whose role is to assist smaller businesses to prepare for a quake and the important recovery period.

Sitting at Tilbury Island in the Fraser River delta is a potential threat to the Lower Mainland depending on the severity of the next big quake. This is where huge tanks are located containing liquid natural gas stored at a very chilly minus 265 degrees centigrade. The tanks are well built, erected on a solid foundation and are seismically monitored. Similar ones have not cracked or burst open during quakes in other areas. The company has installed two dykes to provide containment and vapor dispersion studies indicate that venting gas would remain localized. The company keeps a close eye on Tilbury, constantly studying and upgrading the facility.

There is a mutual-aid agreement with eight American gas companies and similar arrangements with other Canadian firms. In the event of a big one, all west coast gas companies have their own first responsibilities and priorities and then would help each other.

It's smart to take time to learn about home measures that don't cost much, and if the insurance industry gets its way, would cut earthquake premiums. These points were also emphasized: don't turn off the gas unless you can smell it or the venting is obviously damaged, don't try to relight it yourself, and make sure that everything possible is strapped up or tied down before the next one rolls along.

GOING WITHOUT ELECTRICITY

In each of its major locations in the Lower Mainland, Vancouver Island and the North Coast, B.C. Hydro has located white cabinets about a metre square that are bolted to the floor. In high occupancy locations one can be found on every floor of a building. Inside are emergency supplies, bottled water, packaged food, first-aid equipment, a flashlight and three days of emergency supplies for between 10 and 75 people depending on the location. On one cabinet at the Burnaby facility some wag has written — "Shake well before opening." Without doubt, a sense of humor wouldn't be out of place in the sea of anxiety that follows a shake.

B.C. Hydro is the main source of electricity, for light, heat and power that keeps the Lower Mainland functioning. It draws its energy from water that runs down mountains to fill lakes and reservoirs formed by dams operating at 43 sites. Getting power to the Lower Mainland is a complicated business. Unfortunately, it's a system that is highly vulnerable to the movement and twisting of the earth. A major quake would mean that parts of the region could be without power for days or weeks. How long it would be depends on the extent of damage and the many problems hard-pressed repair crews encountered in their efforts to relight the world. The unsightly and much-unloved hydro towers that march across the land are a necessary component of the system. A major problem in bringing power to the Lower Mainland, however, is that towers located on the banks of the Fraser and some other locations are built on land which is susceptible to liquefaction. Extra pilings and steel cables eight to ten centimetres in diameter are intended to help the system withstand howling gales up to 150-kilometres-an-hour, but a major upheaval of the ground is something else again. They may not be attractive, but Hydro maintains it is much easier to repair a damaged overhead system than to find a break underground. Within the Lower Mainland there also are high voltage underground cables running through numerous areas which are susceptible to damage.

Hydro prides itself on the performance of its repair crews. Despite several severe storms during 1994 that affected many parts of the system, customers had service 99.97-percent of the time. The average customer had power interruption for no more than 1.94 hours. The utility responded to 90-percent of its emergency calls in less than an hour, which Hydro boasts is better than the Canadian average. This level of repair efficiency is comforting, but none of these problems compare with those that would result from a large earthquake.

Hydro serves some 1.4 million customers, the bulk of them in the Lower Mainland. Hydro added 42,000 new customers in 1994 alone. It generates annually between 45,000 and 50,000 gigawatt hours of power. Electricity is delivered to customers over 70,000 kilometres of interconnected transmission and distribution lines stretching from 33 generating stations. The corporation spends about $500 million annually on goods and services. Revenues in 1994 were $2.1 billion. It's very big business, and nobody knows better than Hydro that early restoration of service following an earthquake is highly desirable for many reasons, not the least of which is that it needs customers paying bills for service received.

Hydro's 5,500 employees are kept well informed about emergency measures. Plans are constantly upgraded, there's employee earthquake awareness training, and Hydro operates a corporate emergency centre during simulated exercises.

Edward Macdonald is manager of the company's dam safety program. Dams are many kilometres from the Lower Mainland but vital to its everyday life. They are inspected daily, weekly or monthly depending on their importance and key dam-safety indicators are monitored round the clock by instruments. Hydro has never had a dam failure but each one has an emergency preparedness plan which is tested regularly.

The power company has an extensive, province-wide, microwave communications network, supplemented by private telephone, mobile radio and satellite communication links to ensure continuity of critical communications between its control centres and major operating stations. It's essential that the company be able to pinpoint areas of destruction or danger and also to switch transmission routes if necessary.

Despite the fears of some Lower Mainland residents that they could be swept away by massive waters from collapsed dams — particularly on the North Shore — Paul Archibald, the GVRD's senior engineer for water supply planning and operations, doesn't believe this is likely. Both Cleveland and Seymour Falls dams have been upgraded in recent years. Supports for Cleveland's spillway gates and weaknesses in foundation rocks have been strengthened and fissures regrouted. "Cleveland is a large chunk of concrete and not likely to move," said the engineer. Walls to strengthen Seymour Falls Dam were added in 1994.

Archibald noted that there is a popular misconception that dams suddenly give way. This is unlikely. Seymour is a half-earth, half-concrete dam and is monitored for any movement that might indicate a fissure was forming and a breach could develop. Upgrading continues at the reservoir which holds some 25 billion litres.

Since the fall of 1994, GVRD has had its own quake-resistant control centre to keep an eye on the dams. It is manned 24-hours a day and has a secure communications system. Major trouble is more likely to come from one of the distribution reservoirs at Vancouver Heights or Little Mountain, than from the dams on the North Shore. Vancouver Heights holds 6,426 million litres and upgrading to make it considerably safer was completed in April, 1996. Little Mountain holds 11,340 million litres and seismically is unsound. Plans call for it to be rebuilt in 1997-98 in a six-month long project that also will add to its capacity. A significant quake before then could result in a lot of water running down Cambie Street.

Water becomes a very precious commodity in any area hit by a quake and major cities suffer badly from failed dams, empty reservoirs and broken piping. The Lower Mainland is a heavy consumer of water, well above average, with demand increasing three-percent annually.

To Phone or Not to Phone?

With more post-earthquake quality buildings and structures than any other utility, B. C. Telecom is doing its part to ensure communications keep flowing following a major earthquake in the Lower Mainland.

The company is ready, but the population needs practice. The Seattle tremor, a small sample of what is to come, rattled dishes, shook walls, scared a lot of people and worst of all plugged phone lines emphasizing some of the basic flaws in planning and preparedness. Const. Anne Drennan, well known spokesperson for the Vancouver police department, explained some of the problems encountered with the 911 number. She said the 911 centre had 250 calls in 40 minutes after the quake, more than twice the usual number and police response time went up to what she described as "an unacceptable 31 seconds. In a life and death situation 30 seconds is an eternity."

Drennan's biggest complaint was the number of unnecessary calls to an emergency number. Some people phoned just to chat and one individual phoned five times just to ask questions. "Some people should get a grip," she said and described as "highly inappropriate and dangerous" the casual use of 911 to confirm a quake had occured.

B.C. Tel estimated the number of phone calls at up to 10 times the normal level during the hour after the mini-quake. Dial tones vanished because of plugged circuits and a company official described the situation, "like everyone trying to merge onto Highway One at once."

Will your phone work after a real earthquake? Maybe it will, maybe it won't, and how long you're without it depends on the amount of damage sustained. If the central switch for your neighbourhood is undamaged, phone service could be restored fairly quickly. If you live in Richmond or Delta where switching stations may be subject to the vagaries of liquefaction, it could be longer. It all depends on how many kilometres of line are down and there are many, many kilometres that could come down. Power and above-ground lines would be the major concern for the company. Repair

To Phone or Not to Phone?

depends on the extent of the damage and how quickly crews can reach the sites. B.C. Tel has more than 10,000 employees but they would face a monumental task. The Lower Mainland has most of the province's 2.5 million installed telephone lines and at least 150,000 cellular phones. Long distance centres are located in Vancouver, New Westminster and Kamloops and calls can rapidly be rerouted. Said a company spokesperson: "We have a lot of built in redundancy."

Earthquake preparedness planning has been underway at B.C. Tel for a number of years and there are now 21 distinct emergency or business continuity plans in place, based on operations or functioning areas of the company. Plans for restoring service after any major breakdown involve a large number of employees in network operations as well as operator and customer services. Each of these departments must be on-line in unison if things are to work properly.

Rapid restoration of service is the primary objective for the company. Its established priorities include safety of employees, swift resumption of emergency services, and then resumption of regular service to business and private residences.

The company's employee emergency preparedness program is known as BEEP and includes cabinets which contain food, water, blankets and other supplies located throughout major buildings and in higher risk areas. Each cabinet will support up to 75 people for three days. The BEEP program uses "Emergency Wardens" as team leaders and each warden takes first aid training courses provided by B.C. Tel. Many of the educational elements of the BEEP program are available to other organizations and companies for a fee.

New telecommunications facilities are being built to standards which are 50-percent above the building code, enough to give employees and customers a nice warm feeling. Risk assessments are carried out on all buildings on a regular basis and a current seismic upgrade program has been undertaken for facilities in unstable zones such as the Fraser River delta. In the past several years more than $20 million has been spent on retrofitting and upgrading projects. The heart of emergency planning and recovery is the network operations centre which monitors all telecommunications activity in the province around the clock. When there's an outage, the network centre automatically senses the disruption and reroutes calls.

What advice does the utility have for customers after a quake? "Please limit your phone calls, otherwise you will get nothing but a busy signal or slow dial tone."

For business the message is: "Be prepared." Many corporations and municipalities have their own switches and telephones, but many don't know which part they own and which part is the responsibility of the telephone company. The corporation offers advice and training to any company interested in developing an emergency response program of its own.

GETTING AROUND AFTER THE BIG ONE

With the growth of Pacific Rim trade and the promise of more dramatic expansion in the future, Vancouver is now one of the important ports in the world. It plays a key role in the economy of the Lower Mainland, the province, and all of Canada. Improvements and growth at Vancouver International Airport have pushed it to world-class standard with traffic to and from Asia rising sharply. B.C.'s own northern railway, in addition to the national lines, plays a vital role in the provincial economy. Despite the complaints of some commuters, the Lower Mainland has a public transit system that moves hundreds of thousands of passengers a day — by bus, by seabus across the harbour and by Skytrain, a modern, elevated, rail system that straddles the area and snakes underground in parts of Vancouver. Without transportation by land sea and air it is almost impossible to visualize the Lower Mainland functioning in any meaningful way and yet all of the people movers are complex systems, electronically sophisticated, and very vulnerable to earthquakes.

There is a large dependency on electrical power which would be lost for who knows how long after a quake. As soon as it is possible to move people through damaged areas, gas powered emergency vehicles and public transit would have priority. Carrying the most people by using the fewest vehicles is paramount. The private car could be all but ruled off the road and in any case gasoline supplies would soon dry up making the average vehicle inoperable. Transportation companies are well aware of the importance of their role in an earthquake-stricken area. All have emergency plans that are constantly updated. Apart from earthquakes, the companies face a variety of natural hazards and a seemingly increasing number of man-made incidents. Recent subway occurrences in London, Tokyo, Paris and New York, only reinforce the concerns of Skytrain officials who have very detailed emergency plans in place. All major players involved in the movement of people and goods in the Lower Mainland have given much serious thought to preparing to meet the greatest disaster that all of them face.

PORT OF VANCOUVER

Canada is a trading nation with soaring business opportunities around the Pacific Rim. The loss of the Port of Vancouver for even a short time would be a devasting blow to the Canadian economy, although the importance of the port locally and on the national scene is not always appreciated. It's a busy, bustling place, scenically magnificent and always impressive.

It's Canada's largest port, the third largest in North America in terms of tonnage, ranking behind only South Louisiana and Houston, Texas. In 1995, 71.5 million tonnes of cargo went through Vancouver's 20 terminals. That's 25-percent of Canada's total international marine trade. There are 65 shipping berths located at the terminals which sprawl over more than 275 kilometres of coastline, including the coal port at Robert's Bank.

More than 17,300 citizens earn about $700 million annually in wages and benefits handling cargo and passengers, and port businesses and employees pay about $520 million in taxes and other contributions annually to all levels of govenment. It is a major player for all the 62,000 Canadians employed producing, transporting or using the cargo shipped through its terminals. The port receives about 10,000 vessels each year. Highly visible in recent years have been the cruise liners that ply the Alaska run from May to October. In 1995 they brought close to 600,000 tourists to Vancouver who embarked on some 25 ships operated by 12 different cruise ship lines. Growth to 640,000 was expected in 1996. Economic benefit to the port was $40 million. The passengers who came to Vancouver also spent a considerable amount in restaurants, stores and on other services to the tune of many millions of dollars.

On the down side, the port is highly vulnerable to a major earthquake. Despite modernization much of it is old and most of the grain terminals were built between 1916 and 1926. A seismic study shows that of 10 buildings surveyed in the port complex, seven would likely collapse during a major earthquake.

GETTING AROUND AFTER THE BIG ONE

In Kobe, damage to port facilities was severe

Port authorities are well aware of the situation and recently have retrofitted the main overpasses at Heatley, Main, and Renfrew streets without which much business would cease. The potential problems are formidable, particularly the blockage of First Narrows by the collapse of the Lion's Gate Bridge.

The man coordinating the corporation's emergency response is Captain Chris Badger, who stated that the port's main considerations are the preservation of life and property and resumption of business. Many of the port's 65 berths are built on land fill, but some are built on piles which should react better to ground movement than did the docks at Kobe. Canada Place, the show piece of the harbour which combines a luxury hotel, a convention centre and cruise ship facilities, was built strictly to the latest building code in the mid 1980s with extra long pilings driven down to the solid sea bed.

All departments within the corporation are involved in the port's emergency response plan, including the 35 members of Ports Canada police who work in close liaison with local police departments. In battling the fires that would rage along the waterfront following a quake, harbour authorities would depend heavily on the five fire boats that are available.

Captain Badger said because of the nature of port business, the corporation is well versed in emergencies of all kinds although a major earthquake would be of a magnitude never before experienced. "We know that communication is the key," said Badger. "Our people must continue to carry out their usual tasks but they must do them quicker and 24 hours a day." The plan calls for an emergency operations centre to be set up on the 19th floor of the Port's Granville Square headquarters and alternative centres have been identified in case that building is damaged.

As is commonly the case, money is scarce and the corporation is unable to do what it wants at the speed it would like, but, priorities have been established and work is proceeding on the most vulnerable docking areas first.

FRASER RIVER HARBOUR COMMISSION

The Fraser River at tidewater was the scene of some of B.C.'s earliest development, piers and wharves having lined its banks for about 200 years. Today it is a busy, modern port, a vital part of the provincial economy. It generates annually about $6 billion in business, gives direct employment to some 2,000 and indirect work to another 10,000. It is the main port for the importation of cars from the Pacific Rim and its Annacis auto terminal also handles heavy Canadian-made equipment and vehicles for the export market. In 1995, 164,000 vehicles came into Annacis and about 5,500 cars and pieces of heavy equipment were shipped out.

The two terminals are covered by more than 200 acres of blacktop and that is one of the main concerns of Harbour Master Allen Domaas when he plans a response to earthquakes and other emergencies.

Captain Domaas said the port has been giving serious consideration for more than 10 years to the possibility of a major quake and continues to develop, upgrade and exercise its plans. The objective, as with the Port of

Vancouver, is to restore service as quickly as possible. Fortunately, much of the Fraser River facility is fairly new, in the 25 to 30-year range. Captain Domaas has been told by seismologists and engineers, however, that strong lateral movement would cause serious damage to pilings at some piers, although others that were driven into the ground vertically would withstand movement better.

"We are planning to build all future structures as earthquake-resistant as possible. We're aware of some weaknesses and are trying to improve them where it is most cost effective," said the captain. The cost of updating such a large facility is staggering and money, or scarcity of it in light of so many other demands, dictates the scope of what can be done.

Much of the port is built on river banks and on ground subject to liquefaction. "If all the hectares of working surface that we have for storage, such as the auto terminal, suddenly dropped a metre then we would have a difficult time operating," said Captain Domaas. Among problems for recovery would be trying to truck in millions of kilos of sand to reestablish the present level of port facilities. This operation would be further complicated by the likelihood that surrounding roads would be blocked and equipment in short supply. The Queensborough Bridge is the questionable link to the Annacis auto terminal and in a major shake its future is unknown. Among the captain's worst nightmares is failure of the bridge resulting in substantial disruption to navigation and prevention of railway access to the terminal.

VANCOUVER INTERNATIONAL AIRPORT

Aboard an incoming jet just metres from the runway or in an aircraft roaring toward take-off is not the place to be when the ground starts heaving and shifting. A devastating earthquake also could knock out traffic control systems. These events are longshots and the odds are much greater that you would be involved in a road accident going to or from the airport.

GETTING AROUND AFTER THE BIG ONE

Vancouver has just spent more than a half-billion dollars on improving its facilities, including a new terminal to cater to growing international travel, a parallel runway to accommodate increased traffic, a multi-level parking garage and other necessities. A federally-funded control tower is state of the art.

The airport has done its best to ensure that the improvements meet and in some instances surpass accepted standards, but there is always the question of juggling stupendous costs against long odds and the fact that in a very severe shake nothing is "earthquake proof"

Officials are justifiably proud of their improvements which point up B.C.'s growing status as a major gateway. Information officer Earle Weichel said the new terminal will be one of the safest places if an earthquake strikes. Its foundation is built on 11,000 pilings, some of them driven 15 metres into the ground, and the terminal adheres strictly to the latest building code.

Figures bear out the key role the airport plays in everyday life. It is a major employer, giving work to some 16,500 and there are many other money-making spin-offs. The 12 million passengers coming and going annually generate more than $3.8 billion, more at the present time than the mining and fishing industries put together.

There are more than 350,000 aircraft take-offs and landings annually at the sweeping 1,538 hectare site on Sea Island in Richmond. Improvements have added 15 gates to the 28 in operation and bring with them a new measure of safety. Fire is a constant threat at airports because of the huge stocks of aviation fuel and other combustible materials. Vancouver's new ramps are equipped with a hydrant system that delivers gas directly to the plane eliminating the need for some of the tankers that lumber around the perimetre filled with fuel. The airport has firemen on duty at all times and its own ambulance service.

There are well-designed plans to evacuate the buildings in the event of earthquakes or other emergencies and personnel are trained to handle everything from fires to terrorism. Because of the need for security, airport authorities are understandably careful with some of the information made public.

Sea Island is wonderfully flat land and just the place for an airport, but it also is part of Richmond, among the most seismically volatile regions in the Lower Mainland. Liquefaction can be expected and damage with it. How badly the airport will suffer depends on the imponderable — the location and size of the earthquake. When liquefaction occurs the ground loses strength and gives way under weight. A site can be strengthened by densification, which is done in several ways, some much more expensive than others. When you put in a fence post or plant a new tree and stomp around it, you are densifying the soil. At some construction sites a heavy weight is slammed repeatedly onto the ground. There's also a mixmaster operation where a vibrator is forced into the ground and supporting materials or pillars are put into the hole. In a process known as "preloading," sand or other material is piled on a site for a period of time so that the weight compresses the ground beneath. The material is then taken away and construction begins.

At Vancouver airport, project engineer Ray Zibrik trucked in two-and-a-half million cubic metres of sand and kept moving it around. A half-million were placed for several months at the terminal building site. When the sand was removed, 11,000 pilings were driven into the ground.

Two million cubic metres were then used primarily for the new 3,030-metre long runway. It was preloaded onto the ground and left for many months before it was removed and the tarmac laid down. Because of the tremendous cost, more expensive densification methods were not used. The improvements meet all current standards and are vastly superior to prevailing conditions at other airports located in earthquake-prone zones. Construction knowledge and techniques have improved dramatically in recent years and are a far cry from the methods used when the airport was built and added to over the last 50 odd years. Much traffic has rumbled over the old runways and they have had lots of time to settle, but how much densification went into their original construction is anybody's guess. Vancouver's air traffic control system is now state of the art and then some, but frightening nevertheless is the thought of a wipe-out of the tower and its back-up systems. Terry Spurgeon, an air traffic control specialist with Transport Canada which has responsibility for handling all movement, underplays it a bit when he says the first 30 minutes after any complete wipeout of the system would be "fairly hectic."

The tower is built to strict specifications and could withstand a major wallop, but heavy damage would bring with it a tension filled half-hour. An incident in March, 1996, at Toronto's Pearson International demonstrated the capabilities, expertise and experience of the people in Canada's aviation business. A power failure at Toronto wiped out the radar system and its back-up, a system crucial at the country's busiest airport which directs about 60 flights an hour. Emergency procedures were put into operation to land approaching aircraft immediately. Some pilots relied strictly on visual flight and other aircraft were diverted to airports as far away as Montreal, Winnipeg and Cleveland. There were no mishaps.

Spurgeon said the aircraft on immediate approach would be the prime concern and then incoming planes within 100 miles of Vancouver. Other factors in the mix would be weather conditions and whether it was daylight or darkness. The specialist noted that controllers and pilots are all trained to meet a wide variety of crisis situations and the latter would be able to talk to other aircraft even if they were out of radio touch with the ground. They would be guided by the normal rules of air and traffic procedures.

Just as aircraft at Toronto were diverted to places as far away as Cleveland and Winnipeg, incoming Vancouver traffic could be handled easily by other airports not affected by the quake. Even smaller airports can accommodate large incoming aircraft because they have burned off most of their fuel and need less landing space. While a major quake at Vancouver International would cause more than enough problems, it seems to be as ready as possible to meet the future.

B. C. TRANSIT

With the anticipated upheaval of roadways, the collapse of highway overpasses and damage to many bridges, B.C. Transit would face chaos after the big one. Few of its 914 buses, 114 Skytrain cars, or its seabuses could be expected to operate normally although some of them would try, and others could be back in operation sooner than expected.

In Kobe overpasses and elevated rail lines suffered severe damage.

Gas and natural-gas powered buses are your best bet for transportation after an earthquake because of their ability to maneuver around broken pavement and blocked streets. If you're downtown, however, you may have a long walk to find one. Drivers won't cross bridges until the spans have been declared safe by engineers and the business district could be all but cut off from the rest of the metropolitan area for some time. Skytrain will come to a halt the moment its sensory system feels the first tremor, and you could spend some time getting to know your fellow passengers before your immobilized car gets the all clear. Transit will try to keep you informed of your situation via the intercom. If there is no tsunami, seabuses will sail until they run out of fuel although the pedestrian overpass which crosses the railway tracks, running from the downtown station to the waterfront landing, may collapse. You're on your own getting to the docking area.

In addition to damaged buildings, fires and disrupted services, the downtown area with its heavy concentration of trolley wires would be a chaotic mass of broken lines and stalled buses left in peculiar places. There are 244 trollies in service and this system would come to a sudden and complete halt. On the Granville Mall trolley buses would be scattered through the intersections and piled up in the usual places, but none of them would be able to move. Fourteen substations throughout Vancouver supply power for the trolley fleet and have done so for many years. And there is the problem — the buildings are old, made of unreinforced concrete, and they're not expected to survive even a moderate-sized quake. Dead trolley buses would dot the Granville Bridge. If you find yourself on the bridge get off. Bridges can't be trusted after a severe shaking.

Bus service from downtown to outlying areas, providing roads are passable, would only be available from the south ends of the Burrard Street Bridge, the Granville Bridge, the Cambie Bridge, or the east end of the Georgia Viaduct. The only direct access to downtown is through the east side of the city, via Gastown or along East Hastings Street. Unfortunately these avenues both go through the oldest part of the city where fallen buildings and warehouses could produce rubble choked roads.

Knowing the problems it faces following an earthquake, B.C. Transit has developed a comprehensive earthquake emergency plan which, given a few more years to implement, will put the transportation system for the Greater Vancouver area in the best shape possible under the circumstances. It will take time because it's going to cost lots of money.

Importantly, all 2,300 bus drivers have completed safety-oriented, first-aid training and have been informed of their responsibilities in the event of a major quake. Each has a copy of an earthquake manual which suggests drivers stay on the job and get people home if they can.

As a general policy transit employees not on the job see to their families' needs first and then head for work, probably to the terminal nearest home. Should the company find itself short of drivers, a backup force is available as mechanics and repair personnel are all licensed bus drivers who can be called into duty in a crisis, though they are not normally authorized to carry passengers.

Bus depots are located in Surrey, Burnaby, Port Coquitlam, Oakridge, and North Vancouver. Two of these, Surrey and Oakridge, are equipped with radio telephones. The primary operations and communication centre in Surrey is a new building completed in 1994 and expected to survive a quake of 6.5 magnitude. All ceiling installations are firmly secured. There is backup generating power and the building itself is constructed to the latest standards. In addition to routing, rerouting, and trying to provide some transportation for a severely damaged city, this centre would, as a top priority, take calls for evacuation assistance from police and fire departments.

The glaring hole in B.C. Transit's earthquake procedures plan, adopted in 1989 but only implemented since 1994, is the condition of the Oakridge terminal. It is the largest garage and repair centre in Canada, but a facility very much in need of care and attention. Rebuilding is on the books, but not for five or ten years. Oakridge is a key facility in any high level Vancouver emergency because it is designated as an operations and refueling centre for the Vancouver fire department. Firefighting equipment would use Oakridge as an alternate staging and dispatch area to handle calls for assistance to fight major fires, rescue people from damaged buildings or neutralize chemical spills. Use of the Oakridge depot by the fire department is a reciprocal agreement. In a high level crisis, firefighters can commandeer fuel for both themselves and for the bus service. Under Transit's regular emergency response procedures, both police and fire departments can take over buses for emergency evacuations.

All but one bus centre have emergency generators which can be put into use following an earthquake. Lacking this equipment is the old depot in North Vancouver. The new centre in North Vancouver, built to house West Vancouver buses, however, does have its own backup power supply. Transit has introduced a methane detection system at Port Coquitlam for the 25 new natural gas vehicles operating out of this terminal under a continuing program undertaken by the company to upgrade equipment and reduce harmful air emissions.

SKYTRAIN AND SEABUS

Skytrain carries about 100,000 passengers a day, about three million people a month. It is a unique, completely automated, unmanned system which operates under one of the most sophisticated control and communications systems in the Lower Mainland. Opened in 1986, it is an essential transportation component through several parts of the GVRD. It is programmed to shut down at the first sign of trouble and a key group of people take charge immediately in any emergency.

Station platforms on the system are constantly monitored on closed circuit television. Skytrain also has public address communications options and a sensory detection system which identifies unusual movement or intrusion. In an earthquake, platform instrusion systems which operate by sensing vibrations would set off emergency braking on trains the moment the first tremor hit the tracks. There are two complete sensory systems involved — the passive Platform Emergency Intrusion System (PEIS) and the Guideway Intrusion Detection System (GIDS). Under normal conditions, three to five people in the Burnaby Skytrain control centre monitor station platforms and the progress of all trains. TV cameras observe passengers boarding trains and entering or departing stations. Voice communications with the cars and stations includes telephone, radio telephone, a dedicated phone line and an intercom system.

The Skytrain Emergency Services Committee, which includes representatives from fire, police and the coroner's office, has developed plans and procedures to deal with systems emergencies such as attempted suicides, hostage-taking, fires or the actions of trouble makers. Often potential problems are prevented by a warning announcement in a station or on one of the Skytrain cars. When this fails to produce the desired result, the station emergency stop system can be activated to shut down any individual train. After an earthquake the control centre could not expect to retain all of its TV monitoring capability and communication with field personnel would become an important issue. All are prepared for this emergency. Each Skytrain attendant carries his or her own hand-held radio telephone and each station is connected to the operations centre by a dedicated line used only for emergencies. An intercom system permits the control centre to communicate with passengers in stations or aboard the trains.

Skytrain's operations centre on the Burnaby-New Westminster border is more secure than most. In an emergency the primary objective is the protection of control room personnel, those required to take action in response to a crisis. The decision to label any emergency as a minor or major event lies solely with them. Twelve staff members have industrial first aid certificates and are well equipped to handle minor injuries. After a major earthquake the centre director would order an immediate rollcall and inspection of the control room. Providing TV monitors are functioning, the next step is an inspection of stations and rail lines. Before recommencing the service, management would form a task force made up of key managers who institute a systems assessment and determine if there is damage. Should TV monitors be out of commission, maintenance crews would make a walking inspection of the track, standard procedure after any breach of the system. Many minor emergencies have given control room personnel considerable experience in dealing with crises ranging from occasional fatalities to stopped, isolated cars full of passengers. Each of these highly-trained employees speaks of a job they enjoy because it is so vital to the safe operation of the system, and their dedication to the task at hand is undeniable.

All Skytrain stations are equipped with emergency power capable of operating the public address systems, emergency lighting and elevators for at least one hour in the case of the older stations, two hours in the newer ones. The generator at the Burnaby operations centre can supply 25 percent of the line's total power requirements for about seven days. Portable generators can be taken to any location where they are required.

If you're caught on Skytrain when the big one rolls along, relax, you're in good hands and everything possible will be done to get you on your way. Skytrain station employees will remain on the job and are trained to protect themselves and others from aftershocks. They will check for listed hazards in their own areas and fire wardens will provide care and instructions on evacuation procedures. There is always at least one attendant on duty and two during rush hour. Most have first aid training as do transit police who patrol locations on a rotating basis. In addition to emergency communications, each station is equipped with post earthquake provisions, containers of food, water and first aid supplies for employees. They are urged not to rush home to their families because of distances and the difficulty in finding transportation. Instead, the company suggests employees stay on the job and it offers assistance with communications to reach family members who may need reassurance that their relatives are safe.

The Skytrain guideway and stations were built in the mid-1980s and early 1990s. According to Hans Zimmerling, the engineer in charge of the original construction, a lot of attention was paid to preparing for an earthquake. All minor shakes recorded in the past along the proposed guideway were studied carefully to assess their type and what could be expected along the line. Then safeguards were built into the system. As most engineers will tell you, they cannot predict when a quake will occur nor how severe it will be, but they can build structures unlikely to come down when one strikes.

Zimmerling said that in a moderate quake everything at Skytrain will be OK and in a major quake (6.5 or more) there will be some damage to support towers such as cracks in the concrete, even pieces falling off, but the towers themselves should not fall. With regard to the Skytrain tunnel which runs under downtown Vancouver, he commented: "It has already survived a number of earthquakes and I feel it is pretty safe." The original Canadian National tunnel, largely drilled through solid rock, was built in the early part of the century and upgraded and enlarged when Skytrain was constructed.

The three seabuses are expected to sail fairly smoothly through an earthquake, even to survive a tsunami. At dockside the 400-passenger catamarans would rise and fall violently, staying afloat provided they were not carried ashore by a heavy sea. Afloat they are highly maneuverable. Piers at both terminals are built on pilings and include a floating section which could weather a good sized quake, but would break up if smashed by a tsunami.

B.C. FERRIES

With a fleet of 40 vessels ranging from the newest at 19,000 tonnes to a tiny island-hopper that carries only 38 people, B.C. Ferries is one of the largest operations of its kind in the world. Numerous former B.C. politicians have argued that passengers should be able to travel free because it should be totally funded by the federal government as a logical extension of the trans-Canada highway reaching to mile-zero at Victoria. Ottawa has never bought this idea, but in the 1995 fiscal year its subsidy was $21 million.

In 1995 the vessels carried 22,409,566 passengers and 8,299,207 vehicles as a vital link between the Mainland, Vancouver Island, and the Gulf Islands. From Port Hardy at the northeast tip of Vancouver Island, the service also operates to Prince Rupert, Bella Bella and Skidegate in the Queen Charlottes.

GETTING AROUND AFTER THE BIG ONE

Verne McKeen is the emergency planning officer for B.C. Ferries. In the fall of 1995 the corporation completed a new earthquake emergency plan. Corporate head office is in Victoria and the plan identifies three alternate regional centres at Swartz Bay outside Victoria, Little River near Comox, both on Vancouver Island, and Horseshoe Bay in West Vancouver. A new terminal is being constructed south of Nanaimo with every care being taken to meet modern, earthquake-resistant standards.

McKeen said the major problem is the obvious one; they can't determine exactly how severe the damage will be although they can make some assumptions. The corporation would not expect to lose any ferries in the straits, although a major tsunami on the West Coast would pose a threat. They do anticipate damage to ships at various terminals and the possible collapse of loading ramps and adjacent buildings.

The main terminal at Tsawwassen is the biggest problem because it handles the largest ships in the fleet as well as providing service to many of the southern Gulf Islands. The terminal, unfortunately, is built on one of the most unstable areas of the Fraser River delta and if a quake strikes in the vicinity the damage is incalculable. The corporation assumes there will be heavy damage, said McKeen, and the terminal will be inoperable. Availability of fuel could be another problem.

B.C. Ferries is well aware of its importance to transportation in southern B.C. and its approximately 5,000 employees are versed in emergency procedures. The emergency program is keyed to the fastest possible reestablishment of service. B.C. Ferries has an extensive, modern, communications system and each ship has its own radio telephone equipment. Knowledge of what is happening throughout the fleet would not be a problem. McKeen said a matrix has been developed that clearly outlines the characteristics of each vessel and identifies alternative terminals for use in an emergency. Not out of the picture is the possibility of offshore loading of passengers in small boats.

GETTING AROUND AFTER THE BIG ONE

B.C. RAIL

B.C. Rail lives constantly with the problems of rolling rock, everything from small boulders to large landslides. The line along Howe Sound past Mount Garibaldi, Mount Meager and on to Lillooet is the worst of the rough terrain. The provincially-owned line frequently removes parts of the very scenic landscape which have fallen onto the right-of-way. Some slides are believed to be triggered by earth tremors. Rob Wheeler knows these problems well, he is the man responsible for risk management and litigation for the company.

Maintenance crews regularly clear rockfalls, handle derailments and chemical spills. The company has two emergency response crews, one located in Vancouver and the other in Prince George. Two trailers packed with equipment and ready for fast action in the event of an environmental crisis are always on standby. B.C. Rail also has an extensive communications network, including dedicated phone lines, battery-operated radios, a microwave system and the backing of its Westel communications subsidiary. While most rockfalls can be cleared in 24 hours, the railway is well aware that a major quake could present problems far greater than anything they have experienced. If there was damage to North Vancouver facilities and the line north was operational, headquarters would be switched to Prince George and cars would be rerouted east from there. If the line out of Vancouver was blocked and other lines leading east and south were ripped apart, nothing much would move out of the Vancouver area. One hazard on the North Shore involves the old grain silos, built on landfill on the waterfront adjacent to CN owned rail line where it connects with B.C. Rail and almost certain to be damaged in a major quake. The tidal flats at Ambleside also could pose problems from liquefaction where the line runs very close to the sea and the collapse of Lions Gate Bridge's northern supports could block the right-of-way.

The potential for disaster along Howe Sound and north to Lillooet is probably greater than B.C. Rail would like to acknowledge. Anyone who drives the route to Whistler paralleling the railway is well aware of the work that has been done in an effort to control slides onto the road and track. "Watch for rolling rock" is a part of life in the area. One site near the Black Tusk area is unstable enough for the engineering community to recommend to the provincial government that residential construction there be banned on a permanent basis.

B.C. Rail owns but has no rolling stock of its own on the 38 kilometres of line which runs from Cloverdale to the Roberts Bank coal loading terminal, where there would almost certainly be extensive liquefaction and major flooding.

The company has gone from being the province's favorite transportation joke to a 2,300-employee operation that is a major factor in moving a lot of B.C.'s exports from the interior to tidewater. Started some 80 years ago with a great flourish and heralded as the tool for provincial expansion, its aging well used equipment rocked-and-rolled its way north fairly slowly. Beginning life as the Pacific Great Eastern (PGE) it was for many years known as the *Please Go Easy* or *Prince George Eventually* and these were the more polite barbs. Len Norris, the Vancouver Sun's outstanding cartoonist, owed the PGE for some of his classic creations — the antics of disgruntled senior citizens as the train rattled through "Tiddleycove" in West Vancouver.

Sitting in his office in the near-waterfront headquarters of the line in North Vancouver, Wheeler recalled the old days and commented that B.C. Rail Limited is now a diversified operation, preparing to build a shopping centre in booming Squamish and other commercial operations at Prince George. Westel, a subsidiary, is a relatively new telecommunications company with the latest equipment, about 180 employees and operations in Victoria, Kamloops, Kelowna, Prince George, Squamish, Terrace, Lillooet, Williams Lake and Chetwynd.

In 1995, the line grossed almost $425 million in revenue, with a $47 million net profit. It hauled 114,000 passengers over its 2,314 kilometres of track, but they accounted for only one percent of income, the backbone being the hauling of export forest goods, coal and other bulk products. Trains can be comprised of 140 cars, each carrying 100 tons.

ON THE ROADS

The Ministry of Highways has an extensive earthquake emergency preparedness plan covering the provincial road network, including bridges and tunnels in the south-coastal region. It calls for an immediate damage assessment of all facilities by engineers and other specialists; the establishment of traffic control to meet the needs of emergency response efforts, and the closure of dangerous facilities to public access.

Consultants employed by the government are required to file initial reports within 10 hours of a major disruption recommending interim traffic control action such as: all traffic to remain open and functional; number of lanes to remain open for all traffic including trucks; lanes open for cars and emergency vehicles only; one or two lanes open for emergency vehicles only; weight restrictions, and when necessary to recommend complete closure. The work also involves the sealing off of damaged sites and establishing detours.

The department keeps in touch with the Geoscience Centre in Sidney for any information concerning the likelihood and intensity of aftershocks. Key managers would make their decisions on additional road closures based on information received from all available sources.

A CODE ORANGE DISASTER

The Lower Mainland has more than 10,000 beds in public hospitals and the majority of the 7,000-odd doctors practicing in B.C. They are supported by thousands of nurses, other medical specialists and a modern ambulance service which includes air and marine rescue equipment. Despite the impressive numbers, the health care system would have difficulty dealing with a Code Orange disaster, when all non-emergency operations and procedures are put on hold, walking wounded are, if possible, sent home, and the entire focus of hospital staff and resources shifts to treating the large numbers of injured involved in a disaster.

The main hospitals have organized an emergency communications system to keep in touch with each other but, as some officals point out, it is incomplete and their ability to move the injured quickly to the appropriate hospital could be inadequate. Two hospitals would be important to the survival of people in the southern part of the GVRD. These are Surrey Memorial Hospital and M.S.A. in Abbotsford, the two main facilities south of the Fraser River not separated from the population by bridges which could be unsafe or impassable.

All hospitals have earthquake emergency plans in various stages of readiness, tailored to their different needs, locations and specialties. Getting patients to them could be the difficulty. Some sites retain old buildings that generally no longer house patients but are used as offices and laboratories. Others do have new facilities or buildings under construction. Hospital management appreciates the need for modernization and for bringing their facilities up to earthquake-resistant standards, but all face the same problem — money, getting scarcer as more squeeze is placed on health care costs in B.C. and across Canada. This is the status of some of the principal institutions in the Lower Mainland.

A CODE ORANGE DISASTER

VANCOUVER HOSPITAL

Vancouver Hospital is the largest in B.C. and is the province's third largest corporation with a staff of 8,000 on 12th Avenue and another 1,500 at the University of B.C. facility. It has a detailed disaster response plan which by the end of 1995 had only two major glitches, the lack of a safe backup water supply for the thousands who are always housed on the premises and the absence of a complete inter-hospital, back-up communications system. Two-way radios are used on site as back-up.

B.C.'s hospitals are not all in a similar state of preparedness. This largest and busiest one, which handles 40,000 acute care admissions and 80,000 emergency vists each year, has moved in part into a newly-constructed, highrise tower built to post-earthquake standards. The complicated department by department transfer of staff and equipment into the Podium, Level One and Level Two, was completed by the end of February, 1996. The rest of the move into the tower is dependent on provincial government funding. The new building includes computerized records keeping and a tied-down power, heating, and water-distribution system that should be second to none, provided there is no disruption in pipes leading into the hospital. Vancouver's Marg deGrace, who is in charge of disaster response, said: "Water is still a major problem and will be the major expense." Needed is an above-ground storage facility, pumps, and new pipes. Many of the older ones at the site are cast iron and will fracture easily or come apart at the joints.

The 12th Avenue facilities are equipped with back-up power which in an emergency could supply much of the hospital's needs. All the old Vancouver General Hospital structures east of the Willow Building will be demolished or designated heritage buildings. The latter are structurally unsafe but will be improved and earmarked for other uses.

The hospital has its own fire response team trained in industrial first aid and security, and some physical plant staff have qualified for confined-space rescue. Their role is critical in any hospital emergency and they have held many practice sessions, but without water, fire control would be impossible.

As with many other Lower Mainland organizations, communication is also in jeopardy. The emergency department is linked to the provincial ambulance service under Emergency Health Services and via this to city emergency personnel and then to provincial officials. The links currently depend wholly on the ambulance radio service and deGrace knows full well that may not be enough should Vancouver be shaken severely. "We need hospital-to-hospital communication and a backup mobile unit," she maintained.

The new building will not house all hospital departments. The labs and emergency department remain in the Laurel building and here carpenters are tieing down anything that might move, as well as checking ceiling installations and lighting.

Patient care goes beyond immediate concerns for cuts, bruises and broken bones, to treatment of heart attacks and stress counselling. Many in Los Angeles who originally were released after minor treatment returned later showing signs of stress. Approximately 23,000 of them suffered signs of anxiety and were dubbed the "walking worried" whose symptoms did not show up until days after the earth stopped moving.

DeGrace said stress among employees can be a problem following any major disaster. It is related to worry about families in other locations and the employee's inability to find out whether or not spouses or children are safe or injured. Health care workers need to relieve their stress so they can function at their highest level of efficiency in the emergency situation. After long hours of tension, hospital workers can become exhausted and may suffer from survivors' guilt, wondering why they survived when others didn't. If the disaster is the worst experience of their life, they may become secondary victims themselves because they have worked long, hard hours under extreme conditions. During and after an earthquake, there is the continuing threat of physical danger.

Vancouver Hospital's disaster response planning began in 1989 and is geared to: "Ensure that the hospital is in a continuous state of readiness to manage a disaster response in order to minimize the actual or potential danger to individuals, (patients, staff, visitors) or damage to hospital property."

St. Paul's Hospital

Standing on Burrard Street for more than 100 years, St. Paul's is Vancouver's venerable, downtown hospital, but patients are now housed in a modern extension which adjoins the heritage site. Older buildings, including one a century old with extensions aged 50, handle only the departments of psychiatry and out patients. The question of the heritage aspect of these older buildings is still under consideration, although the 40-year-old Comox building is half-empty and scheduled for demolition.

St. Paul's operates on a two-square-block site, has 450 beds, and about 3,500 part and full-time staff. Because of its location, the hospital handles a large number of the city's emergency cases. During the hockey-fan riot of 1994, more than 200 casualties were treated for everything from cuts to broken bones.

Warren Hart, chairman of the Emergency Planning Committee, said key requirements for St. Paul's are a secure water supply and specialized staff training. This covers preparedness on the job and also for homes and families because worry can have a major effect on job performance.

Hart said the hospital has frozen and dried food for about 72 hours and some bottled water. Two emergency diesel generators would keep St. Paul's in operation following any major power failure. Security staff and supervisors have some light-rescue training and are equipped with hand-held radios. Nearby Nelson Park has helipad capacity.

A CODE ORANGE DISASTER

An incoming casualty-alert warning puts St. Paul's into its Code Orange procedure which includes operation of its disaster control centre in the new wing. The control centre is in direct contact with its counterpart at Vancouver Hospital. St. Paul's is still refining its emergency plan with specific attention to earthquakes, and expects to have a revamped scenario completed in 1996.

LIONS GATE HOSPITAL

Lions Gate Hospital with 650 beds is the only hospital on the North Shore. The facility in the City of North Vancouver has a main seven-storey tower built about 1960. Technical experts have said that in a severe quake it's likely that two of its lower floors would pancake. A new wing built to stricter standards houses the emergency department, operating rooms, and intensive care unit. Extended care units are in two adjacent buildings

Gillian Harwood, Director of Nursing Critical Care and Psychiatry, is in charge of emergency planning for Lions Gate. The staff of 3,000 was involved in a major exercise in 1993 when 50 students from Sutherland High School played the role of the injured and staff were put through their paces. A lot was learned. It was found that in a hospital evacuation, one-third of the patients could walk out by themselves, one-third could walk out with some assistance and the remaining third would have to be carried out by staff. They learned that carrying patients down stairs was an exhausting task and would require more people than originally anticipated even though special stretchers were used. Harwood said the earthquake evacuation exercise also showed that the walking wounded should leave first instead of last as is normally the case. It was hard for staff to appreciate they should not deal first with the most ill. The emergency exercise revealed that adequate signage was very important so that volunteers could find their way about the buildings. Harwood noted that patients in bed are particularly vulnerable during a quake. Their only protection is to grab a pillow and shield their faces from falling debris.

Lions Gate is located across the street from police, fire, ambulance and the North Shore's emergency operations centre, close enough that runners could be the communications link if necessary following an earthquake emergency.

Planning is based on the hospital being on its own for three days and water, as in other institutions, would be a major problem. Harwood pointed out that Lions Gate, providing its facilities were undamaged, could give major help to the population at large as it has space that could be used for emergency accommodation.

Harwood, with her psychiatric background, is very conscious of the emotional strains that a major disaster brings, and is well-versed in the experience of other communities that have suffered earthquakes and catastrophies. Lions Gate is a member of the U.S. based International Critical Incident Stress Foundation which offers trained personnel as assistance in the event of a disaster. The trauma suffered by some individuals results in behavioural problems such as family abuse, inability to concentrate on important activities, inability to sleep or eat and other abnormal responses.

Katherine McIndoe, psychiatric mental health clinical nurse specialist at Lions Gate, is a member of an eight-person trauma team created originally to deal with staff but which is now talking with police, fire, ambulance and other emergency workers about what services could be provided in a North Shore disaster.

McIndoe learned much at a recent conference about the wide range of problems that affected those who picked up more than 10,000 body parts after a major airline disaster. "The general public is not aware of the tremendous stress on rescue groups and others. The sense of smell alone can haunt individuals for years. They remember the smell of blood and dead and burned bodies," said McIndoe. She added: "The bigger the disaster, the tougher the problem. The reaction can be hours or even months later. People find they can't sleep or eat, get irritable, lose interest in sex and can't concentrate. When people have flashbacks, they sometimes feel they have completely lost it. Flashbacks are among the most frightening things for people to deal with."

The specialist said while some people manage to tough it through, it is essential to tell those suffering stress that it's perfectly normal. "They must be told that the problem is that the brain is trying to make sense of something horrible, something terribly out of the ordinary," added McIndoe. The situation must be explained and people debriefed and talked to, and that is the function of the Lions Gate trauma team. She said it is best to deal with people in groups, such as the crew of a fire truck or a police rescue squad, so experiences can be shared and justified. She concluded: "Trauma would be a major problem after a quake for care givers, rescuers and the general public.

B.C. Children's and Women's Hospitals

Jeff Young, Manager Fire, Safety and Security for Children's and Women's Hospitals, said the site of the old Shaughnessy Military Hospital has its own set of unique problems, many of them related to water. The buildings themselves are located on top of an underground lake which can be seen through the grates in the parking garage. The nearby reservoir atop Little Mountain is one which would likely suffer damage during a quake and so the hospital, literally surrounded by water, could still be short of the potable kind.

"We know we will be on our own", said Young. It was a message received loud and clear by hospital staff following the Los Angeles quake when they watched the devastation on television.

The sprawling grounds off Oak Street, and the nearby St. Vincent's facility, are occupied by a mixture of old and new buildings. Jointly they have capacity for 1,000 patients and employ a staff of 2,600. The former

Shaughnessy Veteran Hospital's A. B. and C. buildings were erected between 1940 and 1945 and are now used only as offices. By comparison, the Children's and Women's Hospital was built in 1980 to the then current standards. A newer research building was completed in 1982.

Infant transport teams operate from Children's Hospital with special ambulances and there's a helicopter pad on the lawn. The 20 security people all have light-rescue and advanced first-aid training. The facility has a large kitchen and stocks enough food for 72 hours and beyond. Its steam plant also supplies Vancouver Hospital, St. Vincent's and RCMP headquarters.

Royal Columbian Hospital

This New Westminster hospital has three main buildings, the oldest constructed in 1963 and now used for offices. The others were erected in 1978 and 1992 to existing codes. Royal Columbian's Ken Anderson said that whenever a renovation is undertaken facilities are upgraded to meet the latest code and all the lights have been refitted. The hospital has 500 beds and more than 2,000 employees.

Emergency officer Don McAllister said Royal Columbian has an extensive emergency plan which includes evacuation routes and relocation sites. It has a contracted security service that is fully trained for emergency work. A UHF radio system is in the hospital network.

Burnaby Hospital

Like other health care facilities in the Lower Mainland Burnaby Hospital has its full share of problems and a scarcity of funds to correct them. The hospital has 450 beds and a staff of about 1,800 to service the community. It's a busy place with some 60,000 cases handled annually by the emergency department.

A Code Orange Disaster

There are three main buildings — the tallest seven-storeys and the smallest four — built between the mid-50s and 1970. All need work to bring them up to modern, quake-resistant standards.

Rick McFadden, the hospital's safety consultant, said an approach has been made to Victoria on the question of funding, but at this time he is well advised not to hold his breath waiting for the money to arrive.

Burnaby Hospital has a contracted security service and a communcations tie-in with the UHF emergency system. Like the other hospitals, water is a big problem. "If we lost the main system," said McFadden, "we have no back-up." The facility has a diesel-powered emergency system with about three days supply of fuel, enough for the length of time that the hospital might be on its own after a quake.

Surrey Memorial Hospital

Occupying a key location on the south side of the Fraser River, Surrey Memorial Hospital hopes to open a new patient tower before the year 2,000. This will provide a new children's health centre and an additional 22 beds for the hospital which is located on King George Highway at 96th Avenue in Surrey. Presently a mixture of new and old buildings, only one of which is new enough to be considered adequate and one dating back to 1958 the sprawling site presently provides 440 acute care beds with an additional 215 for extended care. Staff includes 2,500 people, 1,500 regular staff and 1,000 relief workers. It is one of two major hospitals for treatment of earthquake victims south of the Fraser. The other is MSA in Abbotsford. Major revisions are currently being made to previous emergency evacuation plans.

The hospital has an adequate backup power system and plans soon to have a two-day water supply always on hand. Communications are tied in with other hospitals and a staff person sits on the City of Surrey's emergency planning committee.

A CODE ORANGE DISASTER

PEACH ARCH HOSPITAL

Located in White Rock, this hospital serves a large number of senior citizens living in the area and employs about 1,200 people. It has accommodation for 225 acute cases, 150 extended care beds and has surplus space for another 150. Heather Maxwell is one of those concerned with emergency plans. She said the hospital has had some seismic upgrading and is a combination of new and old facilities. There have been exercises held in the past several years and another major one is to be scheduled. Maxwell added that Peach Arch works closely with the local police and fire departments. Evacuation of older patients in the event of a major earthquake obviously would be a difficult challenge.

MSA HOSPITAL

MSA hospital serves the recently combined communities of Matsqui, Sumas and Abbotsford. If nothing happens before then, MSA will be relatively carefree by the year 2,000 when a brand new facility is expected to open. It has current accommodation for about 200 acute care beds and 150 extended-care beds. Peter Van Wissen said MSA has a very active emergency preparedness committee and has had several exercises. Before the annual Abbotsford Air Show, which attracts thousands of aviation enthusiasts, hospital staff hold a "paper exercise." MSA would rely on the fire department for backup water in an emergency and like the others has its own emergency power. MSA has about 1,200 employees.

B.C. AMBULANCE SERVICE

In a large area that covers the Lower Mainland and extends to Pemberton and Hope, there are 103 ambulances, 370 full-time employees and 800 part-time, said John Phillips, the service's district superintendent. For all of B.C. there are 450 ambulances and 3,600 full and part-time employees. The service has three helicopters and leases fixed-wing aircraft as required.

Phillips said their equipment is state-of-the-art and all training is done at the Justice Institute in New Westminster. He noted that the service's standards are recognized around the world and that B.C. has been called on to assist with training in Hong Kong, Malaysia and other countries. The province has reciprocal aid arrangements with other provinces and with Washington State.

As an example that practice makes perfect, the ambulance service experienced a bit of a crisis following the May, 1996, tremor in Seattle. As the building began to shake, the senior ambulance dispatcher in Vancouver ordered an evacuation because he considered the location unsafe. Taking four other dispatchers with him, he soon resumed operations from a nearby ambulance station.

CANADIAN RED CROSS

The main function of the Red Cross in an emergency is overseeing the registration of individuals at reception centres, the first step in reuniting families according to Harry Gowe, an emergency specialist with the agency. The Red Cross also manages the country's blood supply and would be the liaison with the international community to find additional sources as required.

The Red Cross has 30 staff trained in registration work across the province plus 150 trained volunteers whose main role is to instruct new recruits on how to help in the reunification process. The ability to find out what has happened to family members and friends following a disaster is a vital step in removing worry and stress, Gowe said.

The ability to recover from a major earthquake and the speed and efficiency with which it can be done dictate the entire future of a region and its people. Nothing else short of war can so effect the health, homes, business and industry, jobs, prosperity and all the dreams and aspirations of the inhabitants.

The major problem, experts emphasize, is that not enough has been done by individuals, business and governments to prepare for a quake so that lives can be saved and the Lower Mainland brought back from the ruins more quickly. This is crucial in order to reduce the human and economic loss. There are many plans on the books but too many are uncoordinated and untested.

In one recent large-scale emergency exercise, preparedness officials designed a scenario that called for some 50,000 people to take refuge in a hastily thrown-up tent city in Stanley Park. There would be similar camp grounds for the homeless throughout the Lower Mainland and on Vancouver Island after the real thing. Just one of the many problems would be that among the homeless and injured would be those least able to look after themselves — the ailing and the elderly.

With transportation at a near standstill, treating the seriously injured poses a unique set of difficulties. Under normal conditions each hospital has its own specializations for treatment, but few patients could be moved to the appropriate location following a severe earthquake. Only helicopters have the maneuverability to do the job and there are not enough in the Lower Mainland to move the large numbers that could be injured. It is not unusual for there to be less than 15 beds available to handle serious emergency cases in the whole region at any one time. What would happen in a catastrophic emergency? Hospitals have developed a coordinated approach to dealing with such a scenario but financial restraint is hampering preparedness plans at most institutions.

Consider yourself on your own. Everyone starts by taking care of themselves. The immediate family comes first and then neighbours or others nearby at the time are all that can be relied on when the shaking stops. Semi-organized neighbourhood groups, who pool their talents in order to help each other, exist in some areas and will be a godsend but the cost of coordinating this type of approach hampers its expansion. Experience in California shows that one full-time staff person is required to train and adminster each 100 neighbourhood self-help groups. Each group includes all the families on a block or cul-de-sac up to about 30 homes. No local communities have dealt yet with this staffing issue or attempted to put forward a municipal budget to cover the significant costs involved.

The municipality you live in, its police, fire departments, health care specialists and social workers, will operate according to existing plans, some of which are more finely tuned than others. In most cases there will be an emergency reception centre set up in your neighbourhood at a community centre or other nearby safe, undamaged building.

Municipalities for a long time have been pushing the GVRD to become more involved. The overlord of the area, which employs about 1,000 people, already spends $4 million annually from taxes to run the 911 emergency phone system but was reluctant to take on additional responsibility without additional funds. Late in 1995, however, with the promise of $100,000 per year for two years in additional funding from 20 member communities, the regional authority finally hired a coordinator to study the preparedness and recovery program.

In the trickle-up recovery process, the province comes next and its preparation includes development of the Provincial Emergency Program (PEP) instituted in 1989 and now well underway. The Emergency Program Act was passed in 1993 giving the province sweeping powers in the event of a major disaster, including the ability to declare a state of emergency. The attorney general would be the main player with the power to acquire personal property, control or prohibit travel, order evacuations and ration food, clothing, fuel and equipment. When the job is too big to handle, the province calls on the federal government.

Ottawa's thinking has changed considerably from cold war days when east and west in a moment of madness might have nuked each other. Remember grants for building your own bomb shelter in your basement? The government built its own secure bunkers but has now closed the two emergency centres at Carp, near Ottawa, and at a site near Nanaimo. The cabinet was supposed to rush there in the event of a nuclear attack and run the country from the bunker. The federal government, nevertheless, has a large role to play in earthquake recovery and holds most of the country's money.

Those hoping for a Canadian forces' dash to the rescue with flags flying and drums beating can think again. The plan to close the military engineering school at Chilliwack means that by the end of the 1990s there will not be a permanent military presence in the Lower Mainland. The loss of these engineering skills is a blow. With the federal intention to reduce uniformed personnel to about 60,000 by the turn of the century, there will not be many members available to help in any situation. If the major quake predicted for B.C. also flattens areas of Washington and Oregon, forget about the U.S. Marines coming to the rescue; they'd have more than enough to do helping Americans. In 1995, the province asked Ottawa to reconsider the Chilliwack closure but so far it remains within military reduction plans. The new Disaster Assistance Response Team (DART) announced in early June, 1996, by the Department of National Defense might be able to come to the rescue providing it wasn't already busy on a foreign assignment.

EMERGENCY PREPAREDNESS CANADA

If you are of a mind that the federal government should be totally expert in the treatment of disasters because it has known so many, Emergency Preparedness Canada (EPC) is the organization sitting at the top of the process. David Peters, its Director-General of Readiness and Operations, stresses that Ottawa only steps in when the individual, the municipality and the province can't handle a situation and the call for help goes out across the land.

EPC says everyone should know how to deal with and be prepared to meet any of a list of 60 natural or technological disasters that could clobber the country at any time and admits there are probably more. An earthquake is considered the "Big Daddy" of disasters and some of the catastrophes that government believes could follow a quake in B.C. include: avalanches, floods, landslides, sea and lake surges, tidal waves, dam bursts, explosions, hazardous chemicals in destroyed plants, nuclear reactor incidents (in Washington state), power failures, structural collapses, urban fires, transportation chaos, human and animal disease epidemics, and very possibly civil disorders if victims thought they weren't being treated quickly enough or well enough.

Ottawa has no doubt that seismologists are correct in predicting a quake of catastrophic dimensions on the West Coast. An EPC pamphlet states: "It is expected to have such a devastating impact on the people of B.C. that a massive mobilization of assistance from across the nation will be required to assist provincial and local governments in saving and sustaining lives and protecting property and the environment."

The federal government has a National Earthquake Support Plan prepared in conjunction with provincial plans. Much of it includes coordinating federal departments to play the role you would expect — Transport Canada looking after transportation, public order in the hands of the Solicitor General, engineering and construction with Public Works and Government Services Canada and so on. Two federal laws adopted in 1988 set out Ottawa's position and give it authority to act. They are the Emergencies Act and the Emergency Preparedness Act. In appropriate jargon, the former states: "Whereas the safety and security of the individual, the protection of the body politic and the preservation of the sovereignty, security and territorial integrity of the state are fundamental obligations of government ...." Carefully spelled out in the preamble is the fact that it applies only to a national emergency which is defined as: "An urgent and critical situation of a temporary nature that seriously endangers the lives, health or safety of Canadians and is of such proportions or nature as to exceed the capacity or authority of a province to deal with it, or seriously threatens the ability of the government of Canada to preserve the sovereignty, security and territorial integrity of Canada, and cannot be effectively dealt with under any other law of Canada."

EPC reports to the Department of National Defence and is a shadow of the organization which existed when the cold war was at its chilliest and civil defence was a priority item. Since then it has shrunk to about 90 persons and this number is expected to drop to 80 as more budget cutting bites in. It's obvious that the group is spread pretty thin.

Peters and his headquarters crew are housed in a rather unprepossessing second-storey office on Bank Street in Ottawa. The 1994-95 budget was $18 million which funded headquarters and 24-hour emergency coordination of any major disaster including a telephone hookup across the country. An old army camp at Arnprior, near Ottawa, is now the emergency preparedness college offering training mostly to municipal and provincial officials. Ten regional offices located in the 10 provincial capitals are in liaison with provincial authorities, and publications and audio-visual presentations on preparedness are churned out.

Peters said that while the Canadian Forces are a diminishing factor, all of them would be thrown in to meet a desperately bad situation. EPC also would be the clearing house for offers of external aid, which in the first instance would be offered by foreign countries through Canada's External Affairs Department.

Through ongoing consultation, EPC and the U.S. Federal Emergency Management Agency oversee a multitude of common issues and interests in preparedness. This has resulted in an agreement with U.S. search and rescue specialists to provide people and equipment for B.C. in the event of an earthquake emergency. Vancouver is creating one urban, heavy-rescue team and there are 24 others in the U.S. including one in Washington State and eight in California with one each in Nevada, Utah, Colorado, Arizona and New Mexico. B.C. might have to wait in line, however, if a subduction quake also affected Washington. Help from the U.S. is an interim step while Ottawa establishes two specialized, 60-person rescue teams of its own which will be made up of firefighters, soldiers and engineers. One likely will be located in Alberta to serve Western Canada and the other in Ontario to service the East.

EPC staff represents Canada on the NATO Senior Civil Emergency Planning Committee and the NATO Civil Defence Committee. Now that the cold war is kaput, there are even links with Eastern European countries on the subject although it's a trifle difficult to determine exactly what use they are.

In addition to dispensing earthquake pamphlets such as Emergency Preparedness for Seniors — 91-percent of the 2.4 million Canadians aged 65 or over live at home — Ottawa backs up its good intentions with some money. EPC administers Disaster Financial Assistance arrangements. Between 1970 and 1995, under fairly stringent guidelines the federal government paid out more than $212 million to help provinces meet the costs of disasters. Ottawa responds to a provincial or territorial request under a formula based on population. Payments generally are made to restore public works to their pre-disaster condition and to facilitate the restoration of basic, essential, personal property to private citizens, farms and small businesses. Nothing is paid until provincial expenditures exceed $1 per capita of the provincial population. Ottawa then pays 50-percent of the next $2 per capita of local expenditures eligible for cost sharing; 75-percent of the next $2 per capita, and 90-percent of the remainder.

In a disaster involving a population of 800,000 where the eligible expenses under the formula totalled $24 million, the province would wind-up paying $4 million and the federal treasury the other $20 million. The $24 million would be a drop in the bucket if the big one levelled much of the Lower Mainland. Arriving at what constituted eligible expenses would be a complex and contentious issue. There is also the whole question of private insurance, one of the issues that the insurance industry is urging all governments and all individuals to consider in trying to confront the terrible tab.

THE PROVINCIAL EMERGENCY PROGRAM (PEP)

The provincial government is the next step down in the bureaucracy. Until recently Robin Gardner was the "activator for the provincial field response centre," under PEP. This is a mouthful of a title for an operation that Gardner said worked out of a building that didn't meet current building standards located in Marpole near the Oak Street Bridge. Gardner, a short, stocky man, voluble on his topic, was particularly critical of the lack of concern by individuals and various governments and groups about "mitigation" — preemptive action, taking measures now that could mean the difference between life and death later, and would also speed recovery.

"There is no centralized program dealing with mitgation. The mandate is not clear," said Gardner, who was equally critical of recovery programs at the municipal level, doubting if some exist at all in any meaningful way. In his view municipal plans were poor, requiring planning for everything from assessment of building damage to publicity and information which must be given to the public. Gardner was encouraged, however, by growing public awareness of the danger. His office received about 1,000 calls a month from people wanting information, many of them newcomers to the Lower Mainland. And that number was tallied up prior to the little Seattle shake in May, 1996.

He said of GVRD municipalities, with some exceptions: "Each needs an overall plan covering how it continues to function and how it deals with industry and business. Many have not thought about their response. There is a 'big black hole' and a 20-second quake could result in a 20-year recovery." Gardner emphasized that plans are relatively useless unless they include well-defined recovery objectives and are practiced regularly. "Sometimes it's like a one-drug dependency on plans and not on programs and practice," he maintained.

Gardner shared the concerns of others that the public places too much faith in the continuation of telephone service in an emergency. "Too many depend too much on there always being a 911 service, which there won't be," he stated. "You have to be prepared to look after yourself, particularly in the first 72 hours and maybe more." Gardner stressed that there are simple precautions that can be taken costing little or nothing. For example, he wondered how many people are sure the spare tire on the car is fully inflated in case it is needed in a mass evacuation over wheel-damaging rubble.

Over in Victoria, David Gronbeck-Jones, a former military man, is the PEP provincial planner. He said with a smile that in California there are 42 people doing his job. If the population ratio means anything, there should be about 10 of him. His office is in a building constructed to the latest code and much is strapped down the way it should be, an example of good earthquake preparedness on the job. Tying down computers and other electronic equipment is expensive. In this fairly small operation it cost the government $2,400, not including stabilizing items such as filing cabinets which can fall over.

Gronbeck-Jones said "there are little clusters of keenness" but many people and groups simply ignore the preparenesss problem. He has a key role in organizing major exercises and what has emerged from these is that some municipalities are not even clear on what resources they have. Preparing inventories should be neither difficult nor expensive but as the planner pointed out, "some people learn the hard way."

The provincial government is also responsible for turning out information pamphlets and lists them in detail on the internet. It is a little unusual to find an official with kind words for the media, but Gronbeck-Jones is one. "The media has been fantastic," he said. "Any time we have done anything to promote preparedness we have had their full support."

EMERGENCY SOCIAL SERVICES (ESS)

How do you care for thousands and thousands of homeless, hurt, hungry, and frightened people? At the head of these efforts in Victoria is Ivan Carlson, manager of Emergency Social Services (ESS) Policy, Planning and Research, for the Ministry of Social Services. He is assisted by Dave Scott, coordinator of the plan, who has organized a support team which includes a long list of government departments and public service organizations. At the community level, Brenda Fox is in charge of ESS volunteer recruitment and retention as well as organizing mobile support teams who can travel to any community to meet the needs of evacuees during an emergency.

Carlson's office has a sweeping view of Victoria Harbour and the legislature but the building is old and built on fill, a good place to stay away from in the event of a shake. His policies and plans now cover 160 communities and 3,577 registered volunteers. To achieve his ultimate goal which is to provide for the immediate needs of families forced from their homes by emergencies and to give them time to begin working towards recovery, Carlson turned to experts in various fields and in many provincial government departments for assistance. He said Scott is an essential player who has brought together a whole group of organizations to be a part of the earthquake response team. The B.C. Housing Management Commission looks after disaster shelter management, utilizing everything from schools and community centres to church basements and tent cities. It operates a computerized, province-wide billeting system which originated with Expo 86 in Vancouver and is maintained on a continuing basis. The B.C. Restaurant Association with 2,600 members is ready to help feed people, but it does not have the ability to coordinate the collection and distribution of food so the provincial Ministry of Agriculture was called in as the appropriate agency to handle the delivery of food and water. The B.C. Purchasing Commission was designated to collect clothing and blankets when local supplies become exhausted. Moving supplies and equipment around is the logistics responsibility of the Ministry of Forests. During a mock exercise in Stanley Park in 1994, this included providing water secured by the Ministry of Agriculture for up to 50,000 people camped there.

Several communities in the Lower Mainland have plans to establish emergency reception centres. Six are targeted in Vancouver, 12 in Richmond and there is a need for many more. In what would seem to be an understatement, Carlson noted that "there is a real skill in operating one of these emergency shelters." Dealing with shocked, stunned people in the thousands obviously is a massive task and training is the key to handling these difficult situations. ESS training is centred at the Justice Institute where a recently expanded program will provide double the number of courses available in previous years. Sally Pollock specializes in emergency social services training, Ross McIntyre supervises business recovery and John Oakley, formerly with the City of Vancouver, is introducing a program to organize neighborhood self-help groups and another for heavy rescue training. Colleen Vaughan, a provincial employee, trains ministry staff to assist ESS volunteers in planning and response activities.

Carlson stated: "The ESS programs are based on sharing the responsibility and the whole-hearted participation by so many wonderful organizations and individuals is gratifying."

Pollock said her objective was to ensure that every B.C. community has the capacity to provide services for residents, for those in the surrounding area, and for evacuees from other communities when required. Volunteers set up emergency shelters, provide personal services and get emergency reception centres up and running so that those who want to help or who come in seeking aid can be accommodated. The program started from scratch in 1990 and has progressed steadily.

In the U.S. all emergency services are handled by the Red Cross. In Canada registration is the responsibility of Health Canada, but "the Red Cross is a major player," Pollock added. "People are trained by them to ask the right questions, to utilize the talents of volunteers and to provide food, temporary lodging, clothing, blankets, and even personal and emotional counselling."

Financial service coordinators from the ministry have been trained to work with volunteers to oversee the processing of bills and unusual expenditures required during evacuations.

All of ESS has access to a secure communications system which connects them with and is available to emergency social service teams. Telephone Pioneers Amateur Radio Club members have designed and implemented what is known as the B.C. Digital Emergency Services Network which includes voice and computer communication without the use of a standard telephone or regular electrical wiring.

Says Bryan Farrar, communications coordinator, "We are installing radio telephone communications which in addition to voice transmission includes a setup known as 'packet' which is similar to a modum on a personal computer and enables us to communicate via our own computer network." Installed through the Fraser Valley with an objective of reaching as far as Kelowna, Vernon and Kamloops by the fall of 1996, the network was put together by club members and is supported by B.C. Tel which provides space for the equipment free of charge. Repeaters will eventually be placed in all microwave stations between Victoria, Vancouver and Prince George and up Vancouver Island. Using obsolete equipment donated by the Ministry of Transportation and Highways, Club members have repaired and

Telephone Pioneer Amateur Radio Club members have designed and are now installing an emergency services network for ESS

installed new crystals in the old radios. They are all tuned to the operations centre in New Westminster and are now being installed. All of this was accomplished with an original grant of $40,000 and an expense account for the project leader. Total expenditures have now reached $86,000.

Commented Farrer: "It would have cost millions to start from scratch." The list of contributors is long, but key members of the Telephone Pioneers Amateur Radio Club Project Team include Bill Parkes, President; Farrell Hopwood, Past President; Jim Swain who was the software implementation designer and network system manager and at least eight other radio engineers. The public service project began in 1989 and is ongoing. Recognizing that communications is the key to successful response, Dave Scott has become an ardent ham-radio enthusiast and is an integral part of the ESS communications network.

With secure communications and continuing training available, volunteers throughout the Lower Mainland will be prepared to handle whatever happens in the crucial first 72 hours after a major quake. Pollock noted: "We're currently on a wave and have about 6,500 volunteers in our program. They know pretty well what to do, where to go, and how to help."

Mobile support teams have also been established and are available whenever a community becomes overwhelmed by a situation. PEP picks up travel costs whenever the support teams are required.

The ESS program includes recruitement, training and retention and so it encompasses an extensive public information program complete with displays, and pamphlets and participation in Emergency Prepareness Week. Training involves close cooperation with St. John Ambulance, the Red Cross, and the Salvation Army because of their knowledge in the areas of first aid and counselling. The particular expertise of people in these organizations is essential to the success of the program.

In addition to its competence in first-aid, St. John Ambulance has 700 qualified members to administer first-aid and has sent a questionnaire to more than 5,000 others with training in first aid asking if they would help local teams in an emergency. A computer listing of these volunteers is maintained by the organization.

The Red Cross trains volunteers in registration procedures and enquiry services and operates a personal, disaster-assistance program. It also maintains fly-in teams of staff and volunteers to set up registration and inquiry or to train people, on the spot, during an emergency. In addition it has been given responsiblity for setting up and managing a staffing bureau to plan for the needs of relief workers brought to a disaster area.

The Salvation Army has 125 trained officers, 55 of whom live in Greater Vancouver, and a number of trained lay people to provide personal counselling and other services in an emergency. In the Lower Mainland and throughout B.C. their competence is evident at disasters such as major forest fires or long-term search and rescue attempts where their fully equipped, food-emergency vehicle is more than welcome.

At the Justice Institute ESS offers various courses under three different programs to volunteers who make a commitment to offer their services for two years in exchange for free instruction. There is a five-day directors' program. Headquarters coordinators take a shorter two-day course on shelter management and a one-day program concentrates on team-building techniques, disaster preparedness planning and utilizing post-disaster volunteers.

B.C. is more advanced in this area than other provinces in Canada and there is a growing ESS Association of B.C. Pollock's one-day training package is available from the Association, and there is a regular news letter and an 800 phone number.

Disaster child care was at one time a particular concern to ESS. It was learned, however, that training could be provided by the Christian Reformed Church of the U.S. which operates a well respected, non-denominational service. The trainers were brought to B.C. to ensure that in the event of an evacuation skilled care for children would be available when youngsters were separated from their parents or left temporarily in care while parents dealt with other essential recovery tasks.

In support of ESS the B.C. Psychological Association, chaired by Sandra Yansin, held a disaster workshop in Vancouver for private practice PhDs which was attended by 50 local residents who will volunteer their services after an earthquake or other severe emergency.

SMALL BUSINESS RECOVERY

The heavy concentration of small business in the Lower Mainland and Victoria is particularly vulnerable to devastation from a 6.5 or larger earthquake. This thriving mainstay of the B.C. economy would suffer not only physical and structural plant damage but few companies have recovery plans in place. Many small and medium sized enterprises would die in the rubble; hopes, dreams and jobs unsalvagable.

Ross McIntyre is in charge of the emergency management training program at the Justice Institute. He has informed some 3,000 business people on the ins-and-outs of emergency preparedness and business recovery since the program was introduced in 1989. This isn't enough, however, to save the economy of the region if the big one comes along soon.

"A defining event will affect your life for ten years after it happens," said McIntyre. "My job is to affect some thinking now, before the event, so more business will survive afterwards."

Many small and medium sized businesses in Kobe were ruined, the damage so severe that recovery was impossible

He wants to encourage business to prepare for an earthquake by putting the best minds in each firm into some emergency planning, management and response. McIntyre is also a member of the Regional Emergency Planning Committee which gives him a good overall perspective on preparedness and response for all of the GVRD.

He said the greatest needs are for trained teams to handle both light and heavy urban rescue, and to get more small and medium-sized organizations into the act. "I think institutions and big business have taken a look at this and done some real work, particularly the public utilities but small and medium sized businesses are not ready. Too often they don't see the cost benefit," said McIntyre, "and that's the bottom line."

One company preparing to help is IBM Canada Ltd., which has established a business recovery centre in Calgary and plans one for Vancouver. The centre is for corporations to use if for any reason their own computers are shut down. The recovery centres have about 20 computer terminals and a high-speed communications network — good in a small crisis, but not up to providing for the business needs of B.C. after an extensive earthquake.

In recent years new statistics on business recovery obtained following the large quakes that hit the San Francisco and Los Angeles areas speak volumes. Without continuation plans in place, small business takes much too long to restart. The sudden loss of revenue for weeks or even months spells the end for any who before disaster struck had even slight cash flow problems or staffing shortages. Many small businesses in San Francisco and Los Angeles didn't exist a year after the quakes. They simply floundered and died without key personnel, necessary raw materials or essential information that was lost when computers crashed.

"In downtown Vancouver it could be months before there was a return to normal," McIntyre said. "Business needs to look at its alternatives." He encourages executives to develop a recovery plan which is an assessment of hazards and risks, probabilities and costs, not a bad thing for any thriving enterprise to have on hand. The plan assesses the critical business function and looks at key personnel, major elements, location, computer programs and backup, even how long the business could survive without its key elements. Often a great deal can be done to reduce the risks and to shorten the period until a restart can be achieved.

Some business people are looking at mitigation and beginning to realize that building improvements may reduce insurance costs and that tying down electrical and business equipment is an expense that carries with it a sizeable cost benefit. Many buildings in Kobe were structurally sound after the January, 1995, quake but were non-functional because conduit and piping installed in ceilings crashed to the floor. Even encouraging the tidy office rule reduces the risk of losing essential documents that could make or break a company.

How ready is big business and some of our institutions? Jim Fisk of the B.C. Systems Corporation has developed a program for business continuation planning. It is stored and maintained at the University of Northern B.C. in Prince George, well outside the local earthquake zone. He has also established in Victoria what is referred to as a "hard site," a fairly safe location except perhaps for the big one, for B.C. government systems, backup and storage.

Some of the banks and credit unions centred in the Lower Mainland are moving towards establishing back-up information systems in Alberta. Without functioning computers and cash machines, banks today are essentially out of business. Without banks, business would be hard-pressed to rebuild, rehire or restart anything. Cash flow is essential to the recovery process, finding the ways and means is all part of the risk management emergency planning function.

McIntyre recently took his emergency management planning process to the Women's and Children's Hospitals on Oak Street in Vancouver. With their precious charges and very particular and specific problems these institutions are preparing for the worst.

What of the long-term recovery, the "10 years after a defining event?" Can it be shortened? Yes, if a community and its businesses are well prepared. In Santa Cruz, California, the city planner was finishing rebuilding the downtown area five years after the event. Communities must identify essential services, not only for residents but also for business. Often when repair and rebuilding begin, 20-percent of the repairs will take care of 80-percent of the problems and each community must define its own key services.

Rebuilding the community is part of restarting business and there is no doubt that the 20 cities and municipalities that make up the GVRD are at various stages of preparedness. Richmond and Delta face far different after-effects than do the downtown core or the North Shore. The key elements for recovery are going to be different in all 20 locations and officials do know much more now than they did five years ago. If the big one takes its time, preparedness will be better by the year 2000.

Then there is always the key question about a really big quake. What is it going to cost and where is the money to come from? Financial restraint has affected all levels of life and the lean, mean approach is often necessary to keep small business competitive. But it will require some allocation of funds from local governments and business to take the steps that are needed now to improve the survival rate after the event. Small business and the municipalities are interdependent at all times; after a quake, doubly so.

In the "show-must-go-on" vein for provincial government departments, Steven Butts works in Victoria and is the manager, Loss Prevention, Risk Management Branch, Ministry of Finance and Corporate Relations. He has lots of plans in a very complicated area, the nub of which is the delivery of essential government services to the public and quick recovery from a disruption. One of his tasks is ensuring that government buildings are in the best possible condition to withstand damage, allowing the government to keep operating. Upgrading non-structural building features and securing furnishings are regarded by planners as the most effective preventive measures.

Work is underway in Victoria and elsewhere, with emphasis on securing items such as computers and other essential electronics. Every department has identified the essential services for which it has responsibility and has set priorities. This is an incredibly complicated scenario when some of the details are spelled out. For example how do you get a pension cheque to somebody who may be living in a temporary shelter in a city park? Of course, if the city is devastated and the banks and other financial outlets are out of business, where would you cash it anyway? It may seem incredible to those who use them all the time, but it could be life without bank machines, machines without power and machines without money. Since l992 Butts' group has provided a framework for business continuation planning, the guts of economic recovery.

DISASTER PREPAREDNESS RESOURCES CENTRE

From selling emergency preparedness kits for personal and family survival to handling the conference secretariat for the 1996 international conference in Vancouver on earthquakes, volcanos and tsunamis, the Disaster Preparedness Resources Centre at UBC is taking an ever larger role in providing information on earthquakes.

The Centre began in 1990 with a grant from the federal government in a general awakening to the earthquake threat in Canada. It functions today on a tight budget under director Dr. Henry Hightower of UBC's School of Community and Regional Planning. June Kawaguchi keeps the operation on line and up-to-date.

The Centre gets its money from sponsors, corporate associates and individual members along with support from the university and fees for research projects. Members range from the cities of Vancouver, Coquitlam and Richmond, the Workers' Compensation Board and Transport Canada, to the Centre for Disease Control in Atlanta and the National Emergency Training Centre in Emmitsburg, Maryland. Support from a wide group of interests representing government, business, agencies and the scholastic world is evidence of increasing recognition that earthquakes are a serious global threat, not something away off in the distance, at some unknown time and under somebody else's turf.

Among the Centre's first undertakings were three projects for Emergency Preparedness Canada: Home Mitigation Measures and Earthquake Insurance; Cultural Diversity and Disaster Management and Debris Removal from Disaster Sites. Other work has included completion of volume one of B.C. Hazard, Risk and Vulnerability analysis for the provincial government; an emergency information plan developed for the city of Nanaimo, and a study for the federal government to estimate the total national expenditure on preparednesss and response activity for natural or person-induced emergencies in Canada in 1990-91.

The Centre's library resources include more than 1,300 books, reports, videotapes, slide collections and multimedia training packages in addition to a wide range of other published information. It is working with international groups to increase and facilitate the exchange of information about earthquakes and other disasters. Dr. Hightower stresses the need for information exchange globally: "There are resources waiting to be tapped and enriched by users in the disaster preparedness community." Much of the Centre's attention in 1996 was keyed to the organization of the international conference, which, it was hoped, would increase awareness both at the official and public level through attendance in Vancouver of hundreds of delegates from around the world with a wide range of knowledge, information and experience.

EARTHQUAKE BUSINESS

One person's misfortune is often another's gain. Earthquakes are no exception and there has been an upsurge in new B.C. business related to disaster recovery.

Sales of lumber for reconstruction increased following the Kobe disaster, despite Japanese reluctance to import new building methods and materials. John Powles, a vice-president of the Council of Forest Industries, said that in 1995, B.C. made about $30 million in additional lumber sales to the disaster-struck area. Canadian two by four construction methods paid off and stood up better than those of traditional Japanese design. Powles pointed out, however, that some of the collapsed buildings were 100 years old and it was not always a fair comparison. There is no doubt, however, that the publicity gained has benefitted B.C. business in the Japanese market.

Other Asian countries have watched the Kobe experience and there are hopes of future breakthroughs into new markets, although lack of building codes and ancient traditions are factors inhibiting this expansion.

Since Kobe, two B.C. companies have won contracts to build prefabricated housing for the city. Shelter Industries Inc. of Aldergrove supplied 100 housing units under a $3.1 million contract, and SRI Homes International Inc. of Kelowna received a $6 million contract for 140 Kobe homes. Both companies won their contracts in tough international competition, and fast assembly and delivery were factors in completing the sale.

Safe-Pak Supply of Port Coquitlam has received a contract from a Japanese distributor for 1,350 one-person, three-day, survival packs and an equal number of two-person packs.

F.A.S.T. Limited of Delta, B.C. designs, manufactures and assembles emergency preparedness kits for worksites, office buildings, schools and homes. In business since 1988, its list of customers ranges from B.C. Hydro and B.C. Gas to Vancouver International Airport and GVRD hospitals. Its manufacturing plant at Merritt, a location just outside the earthquake prone Lower Mainland, produces food and water rations with a five-year shelf life.

Founded in 1994, Terra Firm Inc. of Vancouver says in its brochure it is there "for your family and home." It provides services in structural re-engineering, appliance securing, furniture fastening, window safety filming, emergency planning and survival equipment. Its brochure says that since 1990, 72,000 people have been killed in 9,100 earthquakes worldwide.

Another new company in the earthquake business is Counter Quake Services Inc. based in Victoria, a distributor for WorkSafe Technologies of California. B.C. president Robert Laundy said his company has access to the most current, nonstructural restraint products as well as technical expertise for hazard mitigation. This includes devices for steadying desk top equipment, securing filing cabinets and other office furnishings. The company lists the provincial government and Vancouver Hospital among its customers.

The earthquake business is obviously booming.

While the Lower Mainland's earthquake shield has more than a few holes, the area is far from defenceless because of the increased concern of many people and actions taken in recent years. An accusing finger can't even be pointed at either the federal or provincial governments where debt reduction is a critical issue. At various official levels there are dedicated people who plug away in a gradually changing climate that has moved in some respects from apathy to growing interest. The communities also have the backing of some dedicated volunteers.

Warnings from emergency officials have contributed to recent moves to upgrade many facilities in the Vancouver region. Dissected by inlets, rivers and other waterways, Vancouver and its surrounding communities have a myriad of bridges which form a vital part of the transportation system. Vancouver alone has 28 bridges of various types and some major ones have benefitted from upgrading while others are being closely examined. It's expensive. Funding from various sources, municipal, provincial, and federal could total a quarter billion dollars in the next 10 years.

This is a look at the bridge safety issue, including work completed, underway or planned:

Pitt River Bridge — built 1914 — 60,000 vehicles daily, new north section built in 1978, older section renovated, minor retrofitting to north section in 1996, remains under study;

Burrard Bridge — built 1932 — 73,000 vehicles daily, $3 million upgrading awaits approval;

Pattullo Bridge — built 1932 - 67,000 vehicles daily, $11.4 million upgrading scheduled to start 1997-98;

Lions Gate Bridge — built 1938 — 67,000 vehicles daily, future undecided;

Granville Bridge — built 1954 — 60,600 vehicles daily, undergoing final upgrading;

Oak Street Bridge — built 1955 — 90,000 vehicles daily, $4 million retrofitting spent, $4 million planned 1996;

George Massey Tunnel — built 1958 — 90,000 vehicles daily, upgrade to be scheduled;

Second Narrows — built 1960 — 108,000 vehicles daily, $7.5 million upgrade begun;

Queensborough Bridge — built 1960 — 60,000 vehicles daily, $7 million retrofitting completed 1995;

Port Mann Bridge — built 1964 — 109,000 vehicles daily, $25 million upgrade starts 1997-98;

Knight Street Bridge — built 1970 — 85,000 vehicles daily, under evaluation;

Mission Bridge — built 1973 — 25,000 vehicles daily, evaluation to start 1997-98;

Arthur Laing Bridge — built 1975 — 67,000 vehicles daily, $4.7 million upgrade begun 1996;

Cambie Street Bridge — built 1986 — 63,500 vehicles daily, no upgrade needed;

Alex Fraser Bridge — built 1986 — 75,000 vehicles daily, no upgrade needed;

Skybridge — built 1990 — 570 trains daily, no upgrade needed.

As early as 1980 a Regional Emergency Planning Committee was formed in the Greater Vancouver area bringing together municipal emergency program coordinators and provincial emergency program staff. The objective was to enhance emergency management, including mitigation, preparedness, response and recovery throughout the Lower Mainland. The committee has expanded over the years and now includes associate members from B.C. Tel, B.C. Gas, B.C. Hydro, Vancouver International Airport, RCMP, Vancouver Port Corporation, Fraser River Harbour Commission, B.C. Ambulance Service, B.C. Transit and Skytrain, and Emergency Preparedness Canada.

The committee has undertaken a number of major programs including: development of an inter-municipal emergency communication system; development of a 12 point position paper on preparedness in the region; sponsorship of an earthquake damage workshop; development of a regional inventory resource, seismic soils analysis and mapping; development of common public education materials and neighborhood programs, and support for the development of the municipal-liaison committee in 1995. The committee also has supported, in conjunction with the Major Industrial Accidents Council of Canada, the development of a guideline document for joint industrial-municipal emergency planning.

This is how some of the larger communities in the Lower Mainland are preparing themselves. This is not a hydrant-by-hydrant count in each area, but an outline of some of the principal problems affecting the different regions and how they are trying to deal with them.

CITY OF VANCOUVER

Until May, 1996, John Oakley sat in a second-floor office in an old building on West Broadway that looks as though it might collapse if you leaned heavily against one of the walls. Since his departure for the Justice Institute, Heather Lyle remains as the city's only emergency planner. Vancouver, a city of 114 square kilometres with a population of over 500,000, has been developing emergency management for some time. The May 2, 1996, Seattle shake that set walls trembling and dishes rattling in parts of the Lower Mainland and Vancouver Island was the only tremor to be felt in recent years, but the city has not been without its share of other emergencies. Among the more recent were the 1994 downtown riot after the Canucks lost a hockey series; the 1995, major fire at the Alberta Wheat Pool that called for evacuation of the Pacific National Exhibition grounds, and various gas line disruptions and chemical spills.

While Vancouver is well aware of the problems and deficiences it faces, some progress has been made on improving emergency response capabilities. A heavy, urban, search-and-rescue unit headed by Vancouver Fire and Rescue Services is being developed and expenditures have been made on firefighting equipment. Capability has been strengthened by spending on increased capacity hoses and three salt-water pumping stations which will be fully operational by 1997. Vancouver is in much better shape than it was a few years ago because of the addition of the new Justice Institute of B.C. in New Westminster for public safety training; the opening of a new tower at Vancouver Hospital, built to the latest building code; retrofitting of bridges and Vancouver schools. Unfortunately, many of the buildings that daily house the city's children are more than 50 years old and need fixing although there's insufficient money for much fast action. Work is planned to strengthen Little Mountain reservoir and increase its capacity. In addition, private companies, utilities and crown corporations have developed new and updated recovery plans.

Contributing to the improvement has been the annual Emergency Preparedness Conference started in 1987 to educate and provide a forum for those involved. The city has identified preparedness as a priority and there are now 3,500 city employees who have received basic training. Earthquake preparedness pamphlets are available in five languages at libraries, city hall, fire halls and community centres throughout the city.

By mid-1995 more than 1,000 buildings had been inspected, mostly in the downtown area and mostly apartment buildings. Engineers walked through old warehouses and commercial buildings but because nobody lived in them they were lower priority for detailed inspection. This is a slow and pricey business. Lyle has developed a list of some 800 volunteers to help provide emergency social services and meet human needs in Vancouver and she has kept on the lookout for organizations and groups with special skills that could be utilized in an emergency.

"Coordination of all services in the Lower Mainland is the key to providing the best protection," said Oakley. He pointed to the communications problem as the big hole in the system and hoped that the proposal by Vancouver for an emergency communications system to cover the entire Lower Mainland area would receive approval. It is generally acknowledged, however, in the preparedness community that Vancouver better not hold its breath waiting for fast unanimity because municipalities and individuals have their own agendas. With varying degrees of candor, the experts say the coordination situation is a real mess, one that can only be fixed with considerable additional spending.

A large part of Oakley's job was education, making the public aware of the horrible possibilities, some of which might be prevented. He said there had been a significant increase in interest, created mainly by the quakes in San Francisco and Los Angeles, and more recently by the devastation in Kobe and other parts of the world. "We couldn't keep up with the requests for information after the California incidents," said Oakley. Preparednesss Week is getting more attention and McDonald's, cagey in spotting motherhood issues worth supporting, is now a sponsor.

Oakley is an enthusiastic advocate of the local "neighbour helping neighbour programs" under development in many Vancouver communities to help prepare the home front for disaster and is now involved in training in this area at the Justice Institute. Every neighbourhood has residents with particular skills and abilities, all of which can be utilized in emergencies. By working together everyone increases their chances of survival and the recovery period is more bearable. In any earthquake, according to neighbourhood statistics in California, 95-percent of rescue and first aid after a disaster comes from co-workers, family members and neighbours. These local self-help groups set up their own disaster plans and encourage individual households to prepare by stockpiling supplies, tying down appliances and securing a water supply. Other communities have also organized this program including the Tri-Cities group of Port Moody, Coquitlam and Port Coquitlam, where some 30 teams have been identified. The North Shore communities are also involved.

VANCOUVER FIREFIGHTERS

While most people have a good opinion of firefighters, these views were recently reinforced in the minds of millions who watched on television as those in Oklahoma City plunged into the shattered federal building to rescue people following a terrorist bombing. In a ruined Vancouver, the city fire department of close to 800 men and women would be in the forefront of coping with disaster, battling flames, trying to stop the spread of fires and freeing people from collapsed and damaged buildings. Fire and safety employees in other municipalities in the Lower Mainland would have their own problems, many of a similar nature, but Vancouver is the heart of the region and its problems would be greater. It has the mass of people, including the West End where one of the highest population densities in Canada is to be found.

One earthquake preparedness exercise was based on the assumption that the downtown area would be filled with rubble, on fire, isolated and largely unreachable, with Stanley Park a tent-city recovery zone. In the downtown core old buildings would collapse into the streets. Granville, Burrard, First and Second Narrows bridges would likely collapse or be damaged and out of action.

Roy Bissett is a Vancouver Fire Department lieutenant with 18 years service. He was appointed early in 1995 to be the first full-time emergency preparedness officer with a particular interest in earthquakes. He was keen and enthusiastic when he first got the job, sanctioned by city hall when it was appreciated that there was a need for such a person. It's hoped he stays that way as he faces a formidable task. He will need all the help and support he can get from city hall, within his department, and from the people whose goose he is hoping to keep uncooked.

The lieutenant is philosophical about the fact that in California they don't like to have a firehall more than 25 years old, while one in his area was built in 1912 and still has a loft for storing hay needed when horses pulled the rigs at a gallop. Over a million dollars has already been spent on this heritage designated building, No. 6 Fire Hall at Nicola and Nelson. Lieut. Bissett said that the department has some of the latest and best in firefighting equipment, but a single piece can cost as much a $1 million, so everyone has become adept at improvisation. The main emergency equipment comprises 24 engines and 14 aerial ladders. All of it is essential if the downtown area is in ruins. Within the force are a total of 778 people, including 556 firefighters in addition to officers and 14 non-uniformed personnel.
Four firehalls, Nos. 3, 13, 15 and 18, are older than most, considered "high risk" and scheduled to be replaced. In the event of a sizeable quake, the old halls and many other older buildings likely would collapse or be badly damaged. It seems absurd to be in the position of having your equipment and possibly many of your men lying under the rubble at a time when they would be needed most. The department is currently developing design criteria for new firehalls. Again it's a question of money.

It must be noted that despite these obvious problems, Vancouver's record for fire dousing efficiency is good — just 50 people losing their lives in fires in the last six years. Fire losses in 1994 totalled $18.4 million and more than a third of them resulted from arson. In that same year there were almost 6,000 false alarms. At any time there are 132 men on duty, with many of the remainder available on call if needed.

Vancouver has many problems for firefighters — areas of old shakey buildings in Gastown and the East End with narrow streets; much of the busiest commercial district squeezed on a peninsula downtown; the West End with its tall buildings and a huge number of cars jammed into a small space; bridges, and mile after mile of volatile waterfront with lumber, chemicals and other export goods piled on the docks, some of them quite old and perched on wooden pilings.

The city has spent a considerable amount on the purchase of five-inch hose and more than $1.4 million to upgrade breathing apparatus. There are two fire boats, backed up by three others operated by harbourside municipalities. Of tremendous assistance will be the three new salt-water pumping stations. False Creek was opened in 1995, with two others at Coal Harbour and Kitsilano Point scheduled to be operational in 1996 and 1997. They are all connected to the new firefighting water system. Costing a cool $7 million each, the pumps relay water through five-inch hose to fire engines and tenders. If water lines in the downtown area are broken during a quake, the salt water stations and fire boats would be the only equipment available to fight fires. Firemen would be able to pump salt water onto any blaze up to a mile inland. A dedicated high-pressure water system also is being built in the West End.

New in 1995 and of obvious growing importance is the formation of a team of 62 people who make up the frontline heavy-rescue squad for all of B.C. The team includes firefighters, Vancouver police, city engineers, building inspectors, Parks Board and B.C. Ambulance Service personnel. It has province-wide responsibility and was formed by the city, the provincial and federal governments with an initial three-year, $625,000 budget.

If at any time there is a need for a heavy-rescue squad anywhere in B.C., this Vancouver team of specialists will be sent in. In addition, all firemen receive light-rescue training which is true-to-life. The biggest problem is acquiring some of the expensive equipment required to achieve a rescue at a large industrial site or high-rise building. At the department's training site on Chess Street, a special tower, a smoke building, a fire building and facilites for teaching the handling of hazardous products are being built. Dogs specially trained for rescue are provided by the Vancouver Police Department's Canine Division.

An aware and prepared public is one of the keys for survival and recovery. Lieut. Bissett stated that firehalls must become "store front" operations, better known to the people they are there to protect. He is pleased with his first venture into raising interest from community groups and hopes to raise awareness in all of Vancouver's 22 neighbourhoods. Volunteer emergency response teams are planned. Vancouver doesn't have auxiliary firefighters as it did during World War II and there are times when civilians could be of assistance to the department particularly in an emergency. Citizens will be trained to assist crews, stretch hose lines and maintain hose streams in emergency situations. Bissett's plans call for everything from speech making to media events, information kiosks and notices, events in schools and community centres in order to enlist the aid of the community when it will be needed most.

Lieut. Bissett leaves the impression that he is not only keen but determined to help Vancouverites meet the great challenge of disaster and have the ability to help themselves as much as possible. Were it that everyone was as enthusiastic.

READINESS IN YOUR COMMUNITY

VANCOUVER POLICE

Vancouver City Police have directed increasing attention in recent years to earthquake recovery methods, just one of the many emergencies for which the department must plan. The force has an authorized strength of 1,080, plus an auxilliary force, and responsibility for emergency planning comes under Inspector Paul Howard. There is close cooperation with the fire department particularly in relation to heavy rescue. Three animals in the dog squad have received special training in rescue and the other 15 are available for similar work.

Attention is paid to particular personal skills of members of the force and Inspector Howard pointed to one member who is an experienced rock climber, a skill invaluable in high-rescue work.

City police recently have turned to computers in a major way. Constable Jeff Peterson outlined what can be expected of the system that was adopted early in 1996. The department is recording data on all its policies and plans as well as lists of inventory and the personal capabilities of its members. The data base will include major buildings in Vancouver and their floor plans, aerial photography and details about important sites in the city. Constable Peterson said the system eventually will enable every duty officer to use his own lap top to access important information about any location to which he responds in an emergency. The files will include similar information from other city services. For example, police will be able to determine immediately what equipment is available at city yards. This computer system should be in operation by the fall of 1997, and the force can then look forward to working from a new, more secure operations centre with its own backup emergency power.

CITY OF ABBOTSFORD

This newly created city, which includes the communities of Abbotsford, Matsqui and Sumas, encompasses an area of 358 square kilometres and has a fast growing population of about 110,000. Mount Baker looms over Abbotsford as an ever-present reminder of the seismic activity which plagues the area, while main transportation links including rail lines and roads cross the flat lands that would be subject to distortions from liquefaction during an earthquake. This could result in chemical and other dangerous product spills. Fire Chief Lex Lexhaagen is the emergency coordinator and drawing up an emergency plan to embrace all of the recently-created city is his main priority.

The district has a diversified economy with rural and industrial activities which include food packing and processing. Abbotsford airport is the alternate for Vancouver International and on a regular basis accommodates light aircraft and small charter companies.

The Abbotsford fire department has a force of 140 volunteer and full-time personnel. Chief Lexhaagen said there is a small but active ESS group in the area and there is a general awareness and appreciation of the earthquake possibilities. The region's schools have their individual emergency plans. The main medical facility is M.S.A. Hospital, an important trauma centre for the region.

CITY OF BURNABY

One of the Lower Mainland's older communities, Burnaby developed an emergency preparedness response program some years ago. John Plesha is the Administrative Assistant and Emergency Program Coordinator for the 168,000 people who live in the city's 92 square kilometres. The emergency operations centre for senior officials is in the Justice Building on Deer Lake Avenue.

Like others, Burnaby faces the question of apathy in trying to get across the earthquake message. Plesha said that well publicized information meetings have attracted only a handful of 15 to 20 people. Nevertheless, renewed efforts to promote emergency preparedness are planned. He is particularly concerned with lack of interest because of the large quantities of dangerous goods that are produced and stored in Burnaby and which travel through its traffic corridors both in and out of Greater Vancouver. He would also like people to be aware of potential water shortages in the event of an earthquake.

Conscious of the fire danger, Burnaby has spent more than a half-million dollars on seismic upgrading of its six firehalls and additional money on high-level ladders for its fire fighting and rescue force of 260. It has a fully equipped emergency mobile command vehicle which cost $140,000 when purchased in 1991. Half of the funds were supplied by the federal government on the understanding it would be used throughout the Lower Mainland. It has already operated at mountain rescues, chemical spills and a hostage taking incident. Burnaby has 54 portable radios for use in the intermunicipal network for communication with other emergency centres, utilities and others utilizing the UHF system.

The city has a major response plan and each department has developed a separate detailed one. The building department is developing another for damage assessment of buildings, including schools and emergency centres. A registry of engineers in Burnaby who could be called on is being completed and the ESS unit has 745 volunteers.

The coordinator said that the majority of high rises built in Burnaby in recent years meet current standards. He is concerned that some of the two and three-storey walk-ups of an earlier vintage might not be able structurally to withstand the effects of a major shake.

COQUITLAM AND THE TRI-CITIES

Bob Lee, the Assistant City Engineer (operations) and Emergency Planning Coordinator for the City of Coquitlam states unequivocally that an earthquake is the biggest hazard facing his city, which covers an extensive 130 square kilometres and has 103,000 residents. He's not sure that everyone of them appreciates this and trying to get home the message is one of his city council's goals.

"Apathy only happens when people don't understand the problem," said Lee. He is an advocate of going one dollar further in any project to make it as earthquake resistant as possible. "If we don't systematically upgrade buildings and facilities we will be bankrupt," said the coordinator. He pointed out just one aspect that is generally overlooked is the combination of the earthquake hazard with other hazards. There are lots of trees in the Lower Mainland and a mid-summer quake when the fire hazard is high could result in sweeping forest fires triggered by gas-line breaks and dangling electrical wires. Lee is highly conscious of the economic loss for B.C. and for all of Canada. He estimates an earthquake in the Lower Mainland could effect as much as 30-percent of the total economy of the country.

Like many other communities, Coquitlam began its earthquake planning in some detail in 1991, consciousness raised sharply by watching California's experiences on television. The City of Coquitlam now is working with Port Coquitlam, Port Moody, Belcarra and Annmore, with a total population of 170,000, as part of what is called the North-East Sector Emergency Program.

The city and sector strategy is focused on the community. The city started the Home Emergency Response Organization System (HEROS) in 1992 to encourage people to take care of themselves. "We need a change in attitude. People need to recognize that there are things they can do about the earthquake threat," said Lee. He added that it is essential to have city staff trained as coordinators who would know how to handle and best employ the volunteers who would rush to help after a quake. Lee emphasized that volunteers need training. Responders can create additional problems if they are not sure what they are doing. "It is amazing the number of people who are hurt in rescue operations. In Mexico City, it was almost one for one," he noted.

Lee is not one who lightly dismisses such events as Emergency Preparedness Week, and has tried to encourage as many local organizations as possible to participate with displays and informational services.

He agrees that communities as well as individuals should be basically self-sustaining for at least 72 hours. Every department in the city has a specific role to play and plans are constantly being refined and improved. An engineer, Lee feels particularly badly that the federal government is planning to close down its military engineering school at Chilliwack which he believes would be a great asset to the Lower Mainland in times of trouble. Lee said Coquitlam's modern highrises are probably best constructed to survive a major shake, but he has grave doubts about older masonry buildings as well as many two and three-storey, walk-up apartments constructed 20 years ago and earlier.

The city has been organizing hazard mitigation for over 10 years. It has spent a considerable amount on modern firefighting equipment for its three new halls and its force of 118. Foster Reservoir, the largest in the city, has been upgraded and work is underway on many other facilities to protect the water system. Water also could be pumped from the Fraser River if necessary.

Communications are expected to be a problem although Coquitlam, Port Coquitlam and Port Moody have compatible systems. Lee thinks the Vancouver proposal for a regional radio system covering all the Lower Mainland is a sound idea. Coquitlam also is planning for extensive use of ham radio operators and their battery systems.

Lee stated that there is not enough information about earthquake fault lines in the area, noting that there is more seismic recording equipment in Los Angeles than there is in the whole of Canada. Coquitlam plans to incorporate seismic equipment in some future projects which he hopes will help authorities identify faults and problem areas. This he considers important because transportation and utility links pass through the area.

MUNICIPALITY OF DELTA

More than 2,500 head of cattle, including 1,700 that must be milked on a regular basis, are among the factors confronting emergency planning in the mainly rural Municipality of Delta. It is 250 square kilometres in area and includes three distinct communities, North Delta, Tsawwassen and Ladner, within its boundaries. Total population is 94,000.

Fire Chief Randall Wolsey is the Municipal Emergency Coordinator and the man with the responsibility for the cows. He is confident local farmers will be able to take care of their stock because plans are in place to deliver food and water if normal supplies are unavailable. Wolsey noted philosophically that it is a problem on the one hand, but a ready food source on the other. Because this area provides food for much of the Lower Mainland, ESS has been able to organize catering from local sources within six hours of an earthquake that will provide 10,000 meals for Delta residents who are homeless or in need. Drinking water, said Wolsey, will come from North Delta Springs which can provide 18,000 gallons per day.

"We're in a better position in this respect than other communities, particularly the North Shore which could be isolated because of failed bridges and so will be limited to the amount of food already there in stores or warehouses," noted Wolsey.

The municipality's major focus for recovery from an earthquake centres on dealing with floods, as well as re-establishing transportation, power and communication lines which run through the area and are likely to be damaged. If this is the case, power to Vancouver Island could be severely restricted.

Some of the chief's concerns, in addition to the cows, include possible damage to the aging Massey Tunnel; flooding and inundation of low-lying Westham Island; flooding and damage to Tilbury Industrial Park; possible destruction of B.C. Ferry's Tsawwassen terminal; and possible damage to Annacis Island.

Dr. John Luternauer, of the Geological Survey of Canada, in his latest report on seismic testing in the Fraser River delta verified some of the main known geological hazards in the district. He particularly mentioned instability and probable failure of the delta slope, and earthquake related liquefaction and ground motion affecting the delta plain. Land near the ferry terminal is probably the most unstable in the Lower Mainland. Liquefaction damage can be expected and would be extensive. Tsawwassen Heights and Sunshine Hills are not expected to suffer severe damage.

Wolsey has established four reception centres for those who require shelter, people have been trained to man them and to provide appropriate services. They are located in Ladner, Tsawwassen, and two in North Delta. In addition to 600 trained municipal staff, ESS in Delta has 350 registered and trained volunteers along with a special team of 96 volunteers who can assess building safety. One major concern for Delta residents is that their hospital does not meet current building standards.

The Fraser River pumping station can provide Delta's fire department of 110 people and five halls with 11,340 litres of water per minute to fight fires which might occur along the river front. Dave Rankin of the Delta Police Department is Wolsey's alternate as emergency coordinator, while municipal administrators are in charge of financing and making political decisions.

Joint exercises held in October and January, 1995, included participation by the Coast Guard, B.C. Transit, B.C. Ferries, Delta police, Delta Senior Secondary School, two major industrial parks and Boundary Bay airport. A school program is well organized throughout the district under a program called Partners in Planning. Pinewood Elementary in Sunshine Hills has won an award for its program, which includes safety boxes housed in old air freight crates that were donated by one of the airlines. Parents pay an annual $5 fee to keep the boxes well stored with survival supplies.

City and Township of Langley

Early in 1996, Langley City and Township joined the slender ranks of GVRD members with a full-time emergency preparedness officer when Sheena Vivian took on the position. The Fraser Valley community covers some 320 square kilometres and has a population slightly in excess of 100,000. It has nine firehalls and about 300 firemen, mostly volunteers. Langley Memorial Hospital has about 400 beds and there are two ambulance stations. The area is largely rural but has some industry, which includes metal processing. Some plants have stocks of chemicals and other substances that could pose a problem in an earthquake, said Vivian. She sees an adequate water supply as crucial although many homes in the area have their own wells. While there are no large bridges within the region there are several smaller ones and any damage to them could result in major transportation disruptions because both the Trans-Canada and Fraser highways go through the district. An obvious priority is the updating of the district's current emergency plan and the organization of a large exercise when the program is finalized. A drive to maintain awareness is one of Vivian's main objectives.

Early evidence of a growing concern can be found in West Langley Elementary School's fund-raising sale of earthquake kits to home owners, a switch on the usual chocolate bar or peanut routine. The drive was organized by the parent advisory committee. Each of Langley's 43 schools has an earthquake program and kits designed for the different needs of students from young children to teenagers. Basic to them are such things as batteries, radios and flashlights. Most Langley schools are in the 25 to 30-year-old range and there has been some retrofitting, although again finding funds is the stumbling block to doing all the work that is believed needed.

DISTRICT OF MAPLE RIDGE

Maple Ridge is a community of 267 square kilometres with a population of approximately 50,000. Don Jolley is the Deputy Emergency Coordinator for a region that for years depended economically on the resource industries of agriculture, fishing and forestry. As it became an important suburb in the Lower Mainland, the industrial base changed to cover a new light industrial mix.

The forest industry still provides two-thirds of the employment in the region and is open to considerable damage from earthquakes. Its sawmills and processing plants are located along the Fraser River on flood plains subject to liquefaction.

Chemical and dangerous product spills are of some concern in industrial areas and Maple Ridge is a main corridor for traffic along the Lougheed Highway and the main line of the CPR which carries an average of 25 trains daily. Pitt Meadows Airport is operated by the Ministry of Transport for small aircraft and has flight schools, charter operations and services for fixed and rotary wing aircraft.

Jolley said the area has an extensive emergency plan and conducted a major exercise in 1992. The region is serviced by a mainly volunteer fire department of 100 operating from three halls. The latest development is an effort to build up neighbourhood groups, and Maple Ridge plans to follow a Washington State program rather than using the HEROS model. Maple Ridge Hospital has about 300 beds and has undergone extensive renovations with an eye to earthquake mitigation.

READINESS IN YOUR COMMUNITY

CITY OF NEW WESTMINSTER

Along with the pride of being one of B.C.'s oldest communities comes the problem for New Westminster that some of its buildings are about 100 years old, built after the great fire of 1898 wiped out much of the early city. Most of the old brick buildings would collapse or be badly damaged in a major shake, particularly those along Columbia Street, New Westminister's main thoroughfare, and the area immediately surrounding it.

No one appreciates the situation more than Mark Gajb, the manager in charge of Risk, Safety and Emergency Planning for the approximately 18 square-kilometre city and its 47,000 inhabitants. He took over the emergency function in April, 1996. "The city currently is developing a seismic upgrading priority plan for some of its older facilities," said Gajb. "With all of the new information continually gained from world disasters we need to update our existing plan."

An immediate goal is to involve volunteers and outside experts to help prepare new plans and procedures. "We need a lot of community effort to make things work," said Gajb, who hopes to introduce the HEROS program soon. It is clear that New Wesminster has quite a way to go and Gajb noted: "We need some time for the plan to take effect and get the resources to make it work."

The city has about 100 policemen and 85 firemen in four halls in the forefront for coping with disasters. Unfortunately the halls are old and need replacing. The present plan is to construct a new modern facility to replace at least one of them on a proposed site adjacent to the new Justice Building.

The city is a busy transportation centre. Skytrain runs on its own new span over the Fraser River but the Pattullo Bridge is one of the oldest structures in the Lower Mainland. Queensborough Bridge, which crosses the north arm of the Fraser, was recently retrofitted at a cost of $7 million.

THE NORTH SHORE

Ross Peterson is familiar with emergencies as skiers, climbers and mere walkers get lost in seemingly increasing numbers while enjoying the great outdoors on the North Shore. The mountains are a magnet that draws the unwary into dangerous situations. Peterson is coordinator of the North and West Vancouver Emergency Program, covering an area of 300 square kilometres with some 160,000 residents as well as a lot more people who cross the harbour recreation bound. He is also the man most often named as an expert in emergency preparedness. His lectures and presentations are often praised by volunteer coordinators and organizers.

Peterson is looking forward to a move into a modern office in the new City of North Vancouver police station, a building being constructed to tough post-earthquake standards to service both the city and district of North Vancouver. On the North Shore are about 300 firefighters working out of 10 halls. Peterson has a fairly sophisticated communications system and appreciates the support of 60 volunteer ham-radio enthusiasts.

Because of the climbing and hiking opportunities on the North Shore, Peterson also has the assistance of a 45-person, fully-trained mountain rescue team with a great deal of experience. His assistant, Laurie Bean, works with 160 volunteers who have trained under the ESS program and would work in an area which runs from Deep Cove to Horseshoe Bay. Following a severe earthquake, about 27 people will take on managerial responsibility for specific buildings identified as centres for information and referral. In the works is an emergency boating group composed of local owners. If the harbour bridges were down or badly damaged, small boats would play a large part in transporting people, emergency supplies and other goods. Emergency docking would be needed and planning would require priority gas supplies for such an operation.

Peterson stressed that municipalities have to be ready to assume the local lead role in an efficient way. He stated that although the provincial government is the senior authority, it could not be up and running fast enough to help at the community level in the first hours after a quake.

One of the hazards on the North Shore is the Canadianoxy plant, a 38-year-old chlorine plant located on Amherst Road in North Vancouver. In recent years plant storage has been reduced but it still poses a problem for the district should the tank rupture and a lethal gas cloud escape into the community. A recent report stated that earthquakes pose the largest danger to neighbours of the liquid-chlorine plant.

CITY OF RICHMOND

Anyone who's lived in the Greater Vancouver area for a few years has heard the fears about what will happen to the 133 square kilometres of Richmond when the big one comes along. It immediately becomes Atlantis West. One recent newspaper story suggested that persistent predictions had convinced some new arrivals who had flocked to the area to seek higher and dryer ground. They and the long-term residents shouldn't believe everything they hear about the low-lying region. For a better appreciation of the situation, the Richmond area should be looked at in some detail.

There are parts of the Fraser River delta that may crumble and fall into the sea, but much of it will not and building regulations in Richmond have for many years been more stringent than in other communities. Construction during the past 25 years has taken into account the possibility of liquefaction. Engineers say that any house built during this period should be well secured to its foundation and is unlikely to take much of a walk, depending, of course, on the intensity of the earthquake. Richmond's newer highrises are built to more stringent standards than buildings in other parts of the Lower Mainland. Densification is a must in order to establish a more solid base for construction. Richmond's Kwantlen College campus was subjected to what is termed, "dynamic consolidation" which results when the ground is constantly pounded by a 16-tonne weight dropped from 18 metres in the air. Other densification methods are used throughout the area. Sometimes a barge-like structure is built on top of the compacted sub-soils before the building goes up. All these precautions are necessary because the land in Richmond will liquefy during a strong earthquake and could drop 30 centimetres or more. Some engineers believe that ground movement from an earthquake will be at least 50-percent more severe in Richmond than elsewhere because when the bedrock beneath the silty surface shakes, the sand will act like jello, magnifying the movement.

Don MacIver is Richmond's full-time Manager of Emergency Programs. He admits that the surface soil is a sand-silt mixture, topped with clay in some areas. That's why the land is so productive and the gardens so beautiful, but beneath that silt is solid rock and hardpan. It's a substantial base

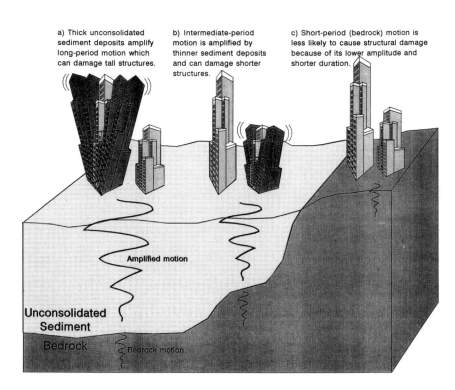

a) Thick unconsolidated sediment deposits amplify long-period motion which can damage tall structures.

b) Intermediate-period motion is amplified by thinner sediment deposits and can damage shorter structures.

c) Short-period (bedrock) motion is less likely to cause structural damage because of its lower amplitude and shorter duration.

Amplified motion

Unconsolidated Sediment

Bedrock   Bedrock motion

for the sandy top layer and while there could be more motion in Richmond than elsewhere, damage may not be great. As a true believer, MacIver commented: "Richmond may be one of the safest places to be in the Lower Mainland. We're better prepared than many other areas."

Dr. John Luternauer, responsible for the most recent study of the land beneath the Fraser River delta, published a map of bedrock based on information from previous studies and an analysis of drill cores made recently. Two 300-metre-long boreholes were drilled on Westminster Highway, one between Garden City Way and No 4 Road and the other between No. 6 and No. 7 Roads. A third was drilled on the current city hall site. Dr. Luternauer concluded that the geology of the delta is far more complex than was previously assumed. The underlying strata is not arranged in tidy layers and the bedrock is not flat but ridged. Silt deposits at the westernmost borehole are 236 metres thick, 200 metres deeper than at the more easterly site four kilometres away. When the delta liquefies it won't shake evenly. There's, however, no question the major concern in Richmond is liquefaction and the shaking will last longer than elsewhere. Dr. Luternauer suggests that future computer modelling of earthquake response for the delta be undertaken in order to identify the most appropriate sites for construction of larger structures in the future.

When this information has been obtained, Richmond officials will know better where to locate large complexes which could sustain severe damage if built in the wrong place.

MacIver and Leigh Bramah, who is in charge of ESS for the area, pride themselves on doing their own thing their own way and their emergency preparedness program is well advanced. This is a unique community within the GVRD both physically and demographically. Compared with the mountainous North Shore, it is absolutely flat and 40 percent of the population speaks Cantonese or Mandarin rather than English. It gives these two emergency planners some unusual problems to which they have found creative responses.

READINESS IN YOUR COMMUNITY

By mid-1995, Richmond had some 400 emergency preparedness volunteers who, in the event of an earthquake, report to one of six staging zones identified within the community. Each zone is equipped with emergency materials and medical kits and two extra kits are on hand for deployment as and where needed. Deputy leaders who are in charge of the zones have all received training and sub-leaders and specialist volunteers are in training.

Between 130 and 140 information meetings are held each year throughout the community, covering personal and family earthquake preparedness. MacIver does the larger meetings while Bramah concentrates on smaller groups and businesses. The local cable TV station runs an earthquake video on a weekly basis produced by the station with comments by MacIver. On request, he will do a personal physical inspection of business premises and make recommendations for improving physical preparedness. He commented: "Businesses need to be prepared for the worst. They must identify key elements and know how best to get up and running again."

One MacIver innovation is a computer software program for use in Richmond schools. Each student and every household within a two-block range of a school is listed on the computer file. It contains emergency phone numbers, special needs for family members, as well as the talents and particular abilities of everyone in the neighbourhood who might be needed by the emergency response teams. Confidentiality is maintained and MacIver hopes that all 58 schools in Richmond will soon participate in the program, which can provide information about the closest and best source of specialty assistance.

Classrooms in future will be equipped with first aid kits, medical cards for each student, and a supply of garbage bags which can be made into raincoats by the students themselves. The kits will include tarpaulins, ropes and blankets, and older students will be taught to dig latrines. Four children in each classroom will be available to take over for any teacher at any time. Students know that if there is a fire you get out of the building. If there is an earthquake with no fire, you stay put.

Another unique program proposal involves the use of stand alone signs at industrial operations which have first aid people on duty. The signs say simply: City of Richmond, First Aid Available Here. They provide helpful information to the general public and are particularly valuable for use by chemical companies and heavy industrial operations. To date 20 companies have agreed to participate in the program. Whether it's an earthquake, a fire or a chemical spill, the signs provide important information instantly — often the key to saving life.

Richmond's emergency operations centre is at Number Seven Fire Hall on Number Six Road. There are seven halls in the city with 230 firefighters. In July, 1995, an additional 41 firefighters from Vancouver International Airport transferred into the Richmond force bringing the total complement to 271.

A 26-foot mobile communication van is in frequent use. It is complete with computers, pocket radios, UHF, VHF and HF radio which is used regularly four or five times each month. The van can communicate with police and is totally self sufficient.

A major issue in Richmond is communicating with the large percentage of the population which has English as a second language. Some have lived through frightening quakes in other countries. Volunteers with language skills other than English are recruited to assist with public displays and presentations, especially those made to Chinese who make up 40 percent of Richmond's newer residents. Volunteers in Richmond receive jackets and badges which make them readily identifiable.

CITY OF SURREY

Jim Bale, Surrey's Deputy Fire Chief and Emergency Coordinator, has some serious, conflicting problems in this sprawling 340-square-kilometre area with a population of 280,000 that is sprouting rapidly. Lack of awareness and understanding are the main problems said Bale, compounded by the fact that a significant portion of the population has English as a second language. Information pamphlets are printed in several languages and much thought is being given to this problem.

Bale is concerned about the housing of many seniors who live in low-rise buildings of older construction. The deputy chief said, however, that many seniors are among those most conversant with the earthquake hazard, including those housed in mobile home parks.

Bale makes public appearances to promote awareness and also utilizes a retired fire chief to speak to local groups. He said a lack of funding by the province makes it difficult to do as much as he would like.

Surrey has two emergency operations centres, one at city hall and the other at Number One fire hall. The area has 17 stations, five new, seven upgraded and the remainder to be improved at a later date. There are 240 career staff and 275 volunteer firefighters. ESS has over 100 volunteers and a group of ham radio operators to assist with communications. Bale noted that Surrey has a new radio communications system that will interconnect with others in his area.

Critical areas of Surrey likely subject to extreme liquefaction are Cloverdale and Mud Bay. These pose particular transportation problems as main roads and railways crisscross the area and there are many miles of secondary roads. Bale has been offered support from the local flyers of untra-light aircraft which would be used for damage reconnaissance and other information gathering. These tiny planes can almost take off and land in a back yard.

READINESS IN YOUR COMMUNITY

CITY OF WHITE ROCK

This small community bordering Washington State has been transformed in the last 25 years from a small holiday resort to a bedroom community for many working in Vancouver and as well has become an increasingly popular choice for many retirees. Sometimes known as Surrey South, White Rock is a municipality with 16,000 residents who live in a 7.7 square kilometre area. Deputy Fire Chief Brian McMurdo is in charge of emergency planning and happy to say that White Rock is one of the most seismically stable areas in the entire GVRD. "We have one of the lowest levels of subsoil in the region," he said. "And under that is solid rock." The only problem might come as a result of sliding in the steepest part of the slope reaching down to the water.

McMurdo, who has two fire halls and a combined volunteer and regular force of about 35, said that while some buildings date well back to the cottage-country era, much of White Rock was built in recent years and is up to current standards. Most accommodation is single or two-storey. A rail line running north and south goes along the waterfront and the only real danger would be a chemical spill if an earthquake struck and derailed a train. With infrequent trains, the chances of this happening are not great. The deputy chief conducts an information program for the people of White Rock and stated there is considerable interest in self protection. The two elementary schools in the municipality — older students go to Surrey High Schools — have their own earthquake plans.

WHERE DO WE STAND NOW?

The small warning shake from Seattle in May, 1996, gave notice of bigger things to come. It's said that nothing concentrates the mind like the contemplation of ruin or sudden death so when walls trembled and dishes rattled a few more people were jolted into awareness that the Lower Mainland is a prime earthquake zone. But memories are short and a few weeks later the little tremor was almost forgotten and who gave any thought to checking personal preparedness?

Emergency officials know from experience that every tremor felt here or televised from around the world — means a few more people do something. Earthquake activity plus education efforts in recent years have helped break down public apathy but information meetings are still called where only a handful show up.

How well is the Lower Mainland prepared? There's bad news and good news. The prevailing view of those involved is that the lack of an integrated communications system for the Lower Mainland and Vancouver Island is the biggest hole in the defensive shield. Experience gained from observing other quakes has shown that without the ability to find out what is happening outside of your own, small, maybe horribly shattered world, rescue attempts are delayed and disorganized — life and limb are at stake. How best to rescue people trapped in wrecked buildings and faced by walls of fire becomes a hopeless task without constant, secure communications. The good news is that a serious attempt to correct this is being made and most of the agencies are plugged in. The bad news is that little more than a plan has been developed and not everyone is convinced it's the best way to go. Some support it and some have opted out. There's also a large cost involved with implementation and construction of a new emergency operations centre. Will an area wide communication system be installed in time? When disaster strikes will those seriously in need of help be able to ask for assistance or will the line be dead and their cries go unheeded? If there is a number one priority this is it.

WHERE DO WE STAND NOW?

Governments at various levels, fire and police departments, and the utilities are now much more aware of the earthquake danger than they were a half-dozen years ago. They are progressing at a steady pace to implement or obtain the items most essential to their particular rescue operations. Members of a heavy rescue team have been identified and it remains only to provide them with the very expensive equipment they will need to do the job.

Most cities and municipalities have plans on paper, a majority are well along in the implementation stage but other plans vary in quality and scope and some experts say that plans without practice are not worth much. Looking on the bright side there's evidence that more exercises are planned on an increased and continuing basis. The experts are hoping that events such as the Seattle shake will encourage people to demand more of their governments in their own interest.

In the trickle-up system which has been introduced, people at the grass roots level are gradually becoming aware of the threat which may shake their home to its foundations and help is now available from the public utilities so anyone who is interested can find out how to secure their own water supply or when to turn off the gas.

Hospitals and health services are being upgraded but almost all of them need a secure back-up water supply. Many hospitals have only a 72 hour reserve. Where that may be enough for a family, it may not be enough for a hospital. Finding the money once again is the problem. It's needed to provide reserve water supplies and for the replacement of obsolete facilities.

Plans are now afoot to increase the number of neighbourhood groups whose members can help each other to survive the first vital hours. School programs are teaching children what to do and how to react in various situations.

WHERE DO WE STAND NOW?

Are we ready? The preliminaries are in place. Some people are prepared and others aren't. What remains are the big important projects — the ones that will cost the most and have the potential to save the most lives.

APPENDIX A — *GEOLOGICAL TERMINOLOGY*

Amplification - When an earthquake strikes it will be felt more strongly in some areas than in others depending on the soil or rock through which it passes. In some situations a resonance occurs deep within the layers of soil which amplifies the shaking.

Epicentre - The position on the ground's surface immediately above the focus is known as the epicentre.

Fault - This is a fracture or break in the earth's crust and a likely location for an earthquake to be centred.

Focus - This is the initial point at which energy is released during an earthquake and is usually many kilometres from the surface of the earth.

Intra-plate Earthquake - This is an earthquake centred at a fault in the earth's crust. Hundreds of them occur regularly in B.C. Most cannot be felt but when they reach a reading of 3 or 4 on the Richter scale dishes will rattle and damage can occur. They are shorter and generally less destructive than a subduction quake, but amplification can cause severe damage.

Liquefaction - When shaking occurs in deep, wet, sandy soil, the land can be transformed into a semi-liquid or fluid mass. When this occurs beneath a building it no longer has a secure foundation, so the structure leans, falls or sinks. This is prevalent along river banks and in river delta areas.

Richter Scale - The size or magnitude of an earthquake is generally measured on a Richter scale named after U.S. seismologist Charles Richter. It measures the amplitude of seismic waves and is recorded by seismographs. The scale is logarithmic, designed so that each number has a ten times higher amplification than the preceding number. Earthquakes with a magnitude of two or less are called microquakes and are too small to be felt. Great earthquakes have a magnitude of eight or higher.

Seismograph - This instrument records and measures earthquakes. Vibrations initiated by a quake radiate outward from the break in the earth's crust. Seismographs detect and record these vibrations or seismic waves on a piece of paper known as a seismogram. These are used to determine the location and magnitude of earthquakes.

Subduction Earthquake - A quake which occurs when two of the massive plates which make up the earth's crust rupture and slide over one another. Subduction earthquakes are larger and longer than the more common intraplate quake.

APPENDIX B — PERSONAL PREPAREDNESS

Following is information from BCTV's Shockwave Productions Inc. pamphlet published by the station as information for the general public following a recent telecast entitled **British Columbia — On Shaky Ground**

New scientific evidence suggests a major earthquake in British Columbia may be closer than you think.

We are all aware of the potentially devastating effects and dangerous conditions an earthquake can leave in its wake.

So if we don't prepare properly, the next earthquake may cause greater personal damage and hardship than necessary.

Although each item listed here won't stop the next quake from happening, it may help you survive in a better way.

FAMILY PREPAREDNESS

Know the "safe areas" in your home and workplace - under a table, a desk or against inside walls. Usually a hallway is one of the safest places if it isn't crowded with objects.

Know the hazardous areas too - near windows, mirrors, hanging objects, fireplaces, and tall furniture. Kitchens and garages tend to be the most dangerous places in typical homes.

Conduct emergency drills regularly, especially with children. Learn your community's evacuation routes.

Be familiar with emergency procedures and policies at your workplace, and at your children's school or day-care. Arrange for someone else to pick them up in case you can't get to them.

Learn first aid and CPR from your local Canadian Red Cross or other community organization.

Designate two emergency "safe sites," one place near your home, and another outside the affected area, where your family can reunite if separated by an earthquake.

Choose an out-of-province friend or relative whom family members can call to relay their whereabouts and condition.

Appendix B — Personal Preparedness

Home Preparedness

Maintain supplies of emergency food, water and other staples, including medicine, a first aid kit, and clothing.

Keep family and personal documents in a fireproof, waterproof, portable container.

Learn how to shut off your gas, water and electricity. Call your local utility now if you have any questions.

Maintain a properly installed smoke detector at all times and affix a portable fire escape ladder for homes/apartments with more than one floor.

Check chimneys, roof and wall foundations for stability, and make sure your home is bolted to its foundation. Call a licensed contractor if you have any questions.

Fasten shelves securely and brace overhead lighting fixtures.

Secure hanging plants, mirrors and picture frames - especially those above or near beds.

Place latches on cabinet doors to keep them closed during shaking.

Keep flammable or hazardous liquids such as paints, pest sprays and cleaning products in latched cupboards or on lower shelves.

Secure your water heater and any other applicance that could move enough to rupture utility lines.

What to do during an Earthquake

Stay calm.

Inside: drop under a table or desk, cover your head and hold on. Stay away from windows, mirrors, brick walls and chimneys.

Outside: stand away from buildings, trees, telephone and electric lines.

On the road: drive away from underpasses and overpasses, stop in a safe, open area, and stay in your vehicle.

WHAT TO DO AFTER AN EARTHQUAKE

Check for injuries and provide first aid

Check for safety: look for gas, water and sewer breaks, as well as downed electric lines and shorts. Check for building damage such as cracks around chimneys and foundations that might pose safety problems during after-shocks. If safe to do so turn off utilities.

Clean up dangerous spills.

Wear Shoes.

Turn on the radio and listen for instructions from public safety agencies.

Replace phone receivers back on their hooks. Refrain from using the phone immediately after a quake, use only for emergency use and only call 911 if injuries are critical.

Lock your door if evacuation is necessary.

EMERGENCY SUPPLY CHECKLIST

Plan to be self-sufficient for 72 hours or longer, and store as much as you can in an easy-to-carry container such as a backpack or duffel bag.

Survival:

Water - 4 litres per person per day

Food - packaged, canned, no-cook, baby food, and food for special diets. Identify the storage date and replace every six months.

First aid kit and first aid book.

Non-electric can opener and utility knife.

Blankets and bedding

Portable radio, flashlight and spare batteries

Essential medications, eye-glasses or contact lenses.

Fire extinguisher

Cash or currency

Extra set of car keys

Appendix B — Personal Preparedness

Sanitation Supplies:
Large plastic trash bags for waste and water protection
Bar soap and liquid detergent
Toiletries, personal hygiene items, shampoo, toothpaste and tooth brushes.
Feminine and infant supplies
Toilet paper
Household bleach and disinfectant

Safety and Comfort:
Sturdy shoes and rain gear
Heavy gloves for clearing debris
Change of clothing
Books and toys for children
Garden hose for siphoning and firefighting
Tent

Cooking:
Barbeque or camp stove, chafing dish
Fuel for Cooking
Plastic utensils, paper plates, cups and towels
Heavy duty aluminum foil.

Tools and Supplies
Axe, shovel and broom
Crescent wrench for turning off water and natural gas
Screwdriver, pliers and hammer
Duct tape, sheeting and coil of 1/2" rope
Matches stored in a waterproof container

APPENDIX B — PERSONAL PREPAREDNESS

For additional information write to:

Provincial Emergency Program (PEP)
455 Boleskine Road
Victoria, B.C. V8Z 1E7

Or call:

Canadian Red Cross:
1-800-565-8000

or your municipal emergency coordinator.

How Would Your Home Stand Up? — A residential construction checklist to help reduce earthquake damage to your home, published by Central Mortgage and Housing Corporation.

Preparing for Business Recovery After a Disaster — published by Industry Science and Technology Canada.

Self-Help Advice on Earthquakes & Earthquake Preparedness in Highrises and Mobile Homes — published by Emergency Preparedness Canada.

Family Preparedness for Earthquakes — published by the Provincial Emergency Program in cooperation with Emergency Preparedness Canada.

Earthquakes in British Columbia — published by the B.C. Ministry of Energy, Mines and Petroleum Resources.

Geofacts - Earthquakes in Southwest British Columbia — published by the Geological Survey of Canada.

Additional information is available from:

Geological Survey of Canada,
#400 - 100 West Pender Street, Vancouver, B.C. V6B 1R8

Provincial Emergency Program,
455 Boleskine Road, Victoria, B.C. V8Z 1E7

Disaster Preparedness Resources Centre,
University of B.C. 4th floor, 2206 East Mall, Vancouver, B.C. V6T 1Z3

Emergency Social Services Association,
#148 - 720 Sixth Street, New Westminster, B.C. V3L 3C5

ACKNOWLEDGEMENTS

The authors wish to thank the following people for their time and patience in explaining the concepts and technical background on which this book is based. We hope that in the end our interpretation of the information is accurate and understandable to the average reader.

From the Geological Survey of Canada
Dr. Garry Rogers
Dr. Dieter Weichert
Dr. John Luternauer

From the Canadian Association
for Earthquake Engineering
Dr. Sheldon Cherry of UBC
Dr. Peter Byrne of UBC
Dr. John Sherstobitoff of Sandwell Inc.

From the Federal and Provincial Governments
David Peters of Emergency Preparedness Canada
David Gronbeck-Jones of the Provincial Emergency Program
Ivan Carlson of Emergency Social Services
Sally Pollock, Ross McIntrye and John Oakley of ESS training
Steven Butz of Loss Prevention, Risk Management Branch

From the Communities
Paul Archibald of the GVRD
Heather Lyle of the City of Vancouver
Capt. Chris Badger of the Port of Vancouver
Earle Weichel of Vancouver International Airport
Lieut. Roy Bissett of the Vancouver Firefighters
Robert Lee of Coquitlam
Don MacIver of Richmond
John Plesha of Burnaby
Mark Gajb of New Westminster
Jim Bale of Surrey
Ross Peterson of North and West Vancouver Emergency Program
Fire Chief Randall Wolsey of Delta
Sheena Vivian of Langley

From the Media
Greg Barnes formerly with CBC Radio
John Ashbridge of CKNW
Bryan Farrer of the Telephone Pioneers Amateur Radio Club
Bill Mackie of Shockwave Productions Inc.

From the Utilities
Ray Nadeau and Mike Davies of B.C. Gas
Edward Macdonald of B.C. Hydro
Dexada Jorgensen of B.C. Telecom

From Health Services
Marg deGrace of Vancouver Hospital
Gillian Harwood and Katherine McIndoe of Lions Gate Hospital
Jeff Young of B.C. Children's and Women's Hospitals

From the Transportation Companies
Verne McKeen of B.C. Ferries
Rob Wheeler of B.C. Rail
Gord Dunning of B.C. Transit
David Sproule of Skytrain

From UBC
June Kawaguchi of the Disaster Preparedness Resource Centre